# EXPLORE
# DORSET
## ITS COAST, COUNTRYSIDE
## AND HERITAGE

# HARRY ASHLEY

With photographs by David Golumb

LOCAL HERITAGE BOOKS

## FURTHER READING

Ron Dacombe and Rodney Legg, *The Dorset Walk*, Dorset Publishing Co.

George Osborn, *Exploring Ancient Dorset*, Dorset Publishing Co.

Sir Frederick Treves, *Highways and Byways of Dorset*, Macmillan

## ACKNOWLEDGEMENTS

The author would like to thank David Golumb, the principal photographer on the project, for his co-operation; the management of the *Evening Echo*, Bournemouth, for the use of photographs from their library; Strangways Estates for photographs of Abbotsbury Swannery and Gardens; Worldwide Butterflies Ltd. for photographs of the butterflies and Compton House; and the Swanage Railway Project for the photograph of the railway. He would also like to acknowledge the help of the many Dorset people who provided invaluable information, including the following who were particularly helpful:
Ian Andrews, Hugh W. Ashley, R.G.S. Avery, Mrs J. Barnard, Tim Battey, J.R. Brady, Tom Burr, Sir Robert Cooke, Ben Cox, S.R. Davey, Lt-Col. G. Forty, John Fowles, Robert Goodden, John Kelly, Rodney Legg, John Makepeace, the Martin family, Keith Moore, Roger Peers, Deborah Ratcliffe, Martin Ridley, Terry Rowe, J. Sales, D.J. Smale, G.M. Smith, A.T. Swindall, G. Teasdill, Captain Thimbleby, Jack West and Don Wright.

The author would also like to thank The Lord Digby, Lord Lieutenant of the County, who kindly wrote the Foreword.

EXPLORE DORSET
Its Coast, Countryside and Heritage
by Harry W. Ashley

First Published 1985
©Harry W. Ashley

LOCAL HERITAGE BOOKS
3 Catherine Road, Newbury,
Berkshire
and 36 Queens Road, Newbury,
Berkshire

Typesetting and Artwork: Publicity Plus, Newbury
Sketch maps by John Baker
Produced through
MRM (Print Consultants) Ltd, Reading, Berkshire
Colour Reproduction by S & M Repro, Basingstoke
Printed by The Guernsey Press Co., Guernsey
Cover Photograph by Harry Ashley

ISBN 0 86368 013 5

The co EXPLO County C the publ

# FOREWORD

By The Lord Digby,
Lord Lieutenant of the County.

Those who explore Dorset will find themselves in a county rich in natural beauty, still unspoilt, and with much to offer, — we, who live here, find something for everyone.

There is the Coastal Path leading from Lyme Regis to Studland providing an opportunity to walk the cliffs, wander through West Bay, find oneself in Abbotsbury, with its famous gardens and swannery, and then along the Fleet Water running beside Chesil Bank, one of the natural wonders of the world. Then you will find the golden sands of Weymouth, so safe for children, or north, the County Town of Dorchester with its traditional Wednesday Market and County Museum just opposite Judge Jefferies' lodgings. Travel to Cerne Abbas to see the ancient figure of The Giant cut in the hillside above the village, and then on to Sherborne with its famous abbey built of local stone — or go east to the steep cliffs of Durdle Door and its deep blue sea, as well as Bournemouth a few miles on, a famous holiday resort. You will pass streams and rivers, ancient manor houses and lovely gardens, you will find churches, farms, meadows, woods, cliffs and sea, all folded in the hills and valleys — because it is Dorset!

Whether you live here, or come on holiday, I hope you will say, as Hardy did, 'Citizens dream of the south and west, and so do I.'

# CONTENTS

The 'Price guide' given for each attraction is simply a guide to the cost of entry.

Cost for one adult:
A: under 50p
B: 50p - £1
C: £1 - £2
D: £2 - £3
E: £3 - £4

Prices may change in the future but the guides should remain a useful pointer to which are relatively dear and which are relatively cheap. As the most expensive sites offer a complete day out with special attractions, the classification is no indication of value for money.

The maps in this book are intended only as a rough guide. For more detailed information the 1:50,000 and 1:25,000 O.S. maps of the area are recommended.

# INTRODUCTION

Where the land mass of England reaches the sea, the southern shore has five beautiful counties, all distinctive in terrain and character. At the centre, flanked by rustic Devon and haughty Hampshire, is delightful Dorset. The rich variety of Dorset soils and landscapes, caused by complex geological strata, are eroded at the coastline into 70-odd miles of bays, beaches, cliffs, ledges and estuaries. There are many clean sandy beaches - popular playgrounds for the children who come in summer — and the phenomenal Chesil Beach, nine miles of pebbles reaching from Portland to Abbotsbury. Poole has one of the largest natural harbours in the world, and towering chalk cliffs, inspiration for poets and authors, grace the Purbeck coast.

The acquisition of Bournemouth and Christchurch as a result of the boundary changes was most acceptable to Dorset. The elegant and internationally famous resort of Bournemouth, with its miles of sands, has Poole Harbour at one end and Christchurch Harbour at the other. These inlets boast some of the country's leading yachting and leisure facilities. Although their identities are jealously guarded by separate authorities, the three towns — Poole with its fishing fleet and cross-channel ferry, Bournemouth with its magnificent hotels and casinos, and Christchurch with its bird-sanctuary harbour overlooked by an elegant priory — form in their entirety one of the finest holiday resorts in the world.

Corfe Castle

Dorset has seaside resorts to suit all tastes. Going westwards from Bournemouth, Swanage is a quaint little watering place. Weymouth, the Georgian royal resort where King George III once slept and bathed, has a busy harbour. West Bay and Lyme Regis are also resorts full of old world charm.

An unkind chronicler has described Dorset as a decaying county and, at one time, he could have been right. Inland, in the farming communities, those engaged in rural industries were a dying race. As many of them retired on small pensions, their cottages fell into disrepair. It was the influx of 'townies' who sought to live in the countryside and refurbished many properties — re-thatching them, modernising and coating them in picturesque pastel shades — that gave the villages a fresh look.

Fireworks at Christchurch

Wareham Quay

Down in the far west, sweet Beaminster way, far from any city or town of importance, life has changed little over the last 50 years. The villages lie in valleys, sheltered by the rolling hills of green. Spring follows winter, through to summer and autumn, but only the weather and foliage colours change. Pilsdon, Trent, Broadwindsor, where once King Charles II fled fled from village to village with Roundheads in hot pursuit, have in no way attempted to forget their past.

That whole western area is very different from the eastern end of the county, where many old villages have become enlarged into dormitories for the busy people of Bournemouth and Poole.

The hilltop town of Shaftesbury in the north looks south across the Blackmore Vale, where Dorset's largest river, the sleepy Stour, twists and winds past the hills of Hod and Hambledon on its way to the sea at Christchurch. This is the gentle country which inspired the Dorset dialect poet, William Barnes.

Further south, the Frome and Piddle wend their way eastward towards the great harbour at Poole, passing through some of the richest farmland in the south. The Piddle flows through Tolpuddle, where the 'Six Men of Dorset' once protested when their wages were cut to starvation level, and were deported for their insubordination. Here also is Thomas Hardy country, the sullen Great Heath which features in his tragic tales. It is now broken by development but it can still be seen at its primitive best between Wareham and Bere Regis.

The Stour at Christchurch

Swanage millpond

Dorset has been closely associated with war throughout the generations. Romans and Danes sailed up the waters of Poole Harbour to Wareham, and the defensive ramparts built by the Anglo-Saxons still surround the ancient town. In 887, Alfred's ships chased the Danish fleet to destruction on the Peveril Ledge, off Swanage.

To title a book 'Explore Dorset' and then proceed to tell the explorer where to go and what to see, could be rather like asking Stanley to find Livingstone and giving him a map to show him how to get there. But this text should be a guide to journeys that will enrich and encourage the reader to seek further and, like Stanley, he will find a lot to interest him on the way.

Mansions with mysterious histories can be visited, and exotic gardens which are open to the public. The country has much more to offer than the well-known places, such as Lulworth, Corfe Castle and Royal Weymouth.

This book will tempt you to seek the beauty and wildlife of the coasts, to roam on the dominating hilltops with their indescribable views, and explore those strange islands of stone, Portland and Purbeck.

The author has roamed in Dorset for nearly 50 years and on every journey he discovers something new. It is a strange, romantic, lovable county where east and west never seem to meet, yet are united in the bond that 'We be Do'set'.

Bournemouth Pleasure Gardens

In the 1939-45 War, Dorset had its finest hour when, in the grey light of dawn, part of the great invading army of D-day sailed out of Weymouth and Poole to meet off St Aldhelm's Head and creep across the Channel to Cherbourg.

Corfe Castle, for all its beauty, has been a place of conflict and royal murder. In 1685, Lyme Regis was chosen by the Duke of Monmouth as the place to launch a rebellion against James II, a cause which was lost within a few weeks at the Battle of Sedgemoor over the border in Somerset. General Wolfe, who captured Quebec in 1759, trained his army on the Hambledon hillside.

Durdle Door

# THE NEW DORSET

Wimborne Minster

Poole

Poole Harbour

Tucktonia

Christchurch

christchurch Bay

Hengistbury Head

Bournemouth

MUSEUMS

# CHRISTCHURCH

The priory stands at the confluence of the Stour and the Avon

Although there is evidence of Bronze Age and Iron Age settlements on the site of Christchurch, the history of the town began 1,100 years ago when Alfred, King of Wessex, set up a series of fortified towns called burghs along the coast as a protection against the marauding Danish fleets. Christchurch, or as it was then, Tweoxneam or Twineham, seemed a suitable site for one of these burghs, situated between Southampton and Wareham. It stands on a spit of land where the rivers Stour and Avon meet, so only the landward end had to be defended.

The Christchurch we know today is one of the most beautiful towns in England, and was proudly taken over by Dorset in the county boundary changes. The whole of its ancient past is contained within a half-mile circular walk.

The great priory, historic focus of the town, has a Norman nave, overlooked by a tower of 15th-century vintage, 120 feet high. The north-east turret of the north transept is a gem of Norman architecture. With its nave, choir and lady chapel the edifice is 300 feet long.

The building displays the workmanship of centuries of craftsmen, and their humour is portrayed in wood and stone carvings, On a capital in the Montacute Chantry, the 12 Apostles are portrayed with a two-faced Judas, and the wooden carving of the fox in the pulpit depicts jealousy between the monk and the wandering friar.

In the beautiful Salisbury Chapel, sit and remember Margaret, the tragic Countess of Salisbury, a victim of the Wars of the Roses. Her father and grandfather were killed in the wars and her brother and eldest son perished at the block. Then her younger son, Reginald Pole, who became Archbishop of Canterbury, angered Henry VIII and the king avenged himself on the family.

The Countess, instead of resting in her chapel, was at 80 years of age taken to the Tower of London and executed.

Christchurch derived its name from a legend associated with Christ the carpenter. The church was to have been built on St Catherine's Hill, a mile higher up the Avon valley, but each day material carried up the hill was mysteriously taken overnight to the sacred site of an older church. Believing it to be divine guidance, the masons started to build on the old site and were joined by an extra workman who was never at the meal table. One day, a beam was cut too short and left overnight. Next morning the beam was not only found to be in place, but slightly overlength. The strange workman was never seen again, and the astonished builders believed that he must have been the Carpenter of Nazareth. The beam is still there but it is not in its original position.

Among the many fine tombs in the church is the Shelley monument. Set up by the poet's son, and depicting Shelley lying on his wife's knee, it had been intended for St Peter's Church, Bournemouth, but there was no room for the giant structure there.

The priory stands at the end of the High Street next to the 12th-century castle ruin, on its artificial mound. The castle was of some importance, commanding a broad view of the countryside, and many battles were fought around it. During the dispute for the crown after the death of Henry I in 1135, the forces of King Stephen captured it from the supporters of Matilda in 1153.

During the next century King John was a visitor, and on another occasion a group of barons met at the castle to formulate some of the provisions of the Magna Carta. The boy king Edward VI spent a holiday there shortly before his death in 1553.

Although the active life of the castle lasted over five centuries from 1106 to 1656 it was described in 1540 as decayed and apparently used for pounding cattle. 100 years later, however, it was used as a fortress in the Civil War, maintained by a Royalist Force. Parliamentary troops captured it in 1644 after a fierce battle in the priory churchyard, now one of the loveliest and most peaceful corners of Christchurch, and in 1652 Cromwell ordered the castle to be demolished.

Close by, and formerly part of the castle, is the Constable's House — one of the most perfect examples of Norman domestic architecture in England. Its image is reflected in that part of the Avon diverted to form a castle moat and mill stream. The house was saved from certain destruction in the 18th century by the Rev. William Jackson, who roused public opinion so much that the ruin was preserved. The walls of the house are almost intact and a feature is the circular chimney.

Other interesting buildings in Christchurch include the old Court House in Bridge Street, which has an attractive thatched roof, and Ye Olde Eight Bells near the priory in Church Street, a gift shop which was formerly a smugglers' Inn. It is dated AD 1450, but that probably refers to an earlier building.

The Convent Walk leads past the mighty priory and gives views of the great tower and long lines of the nave. Nearing the Stour the stream follows a tree-clad bank, where daffodils dance in the spring and are reflected in the water. It is known as Paradise and, from the lawns, resting explorers can watch the stream flow under a two-arched bridge of great antiquity to the wheel of the Priory Mill. Recently restored, it was there in the Conqueror's day. At this point the Town Quay is flanked by a green park. Bands play on the bandstand as pleasure craft of all descriptions pass up and down the Stour.

The Old Court House in Bridge Street

In the late 18th century, there were plans to make the Avon navigable and turn Christchurch into a port for Salisbury. The idea seems laughable today — and may have then — but undeterred, in 1762 the authorities asked the great engineer John Smeaton, who rebuilt the Eddystone Lighthouse in granite, to prepare a plan for improving the harbour and overcoming its shallow entrance. He reported 'I cannot flatter the inhabitants ever to expect a harbour at Christchurch of any great depth or capacity'. So Christchurch remained a relatively poor fishing port, although it engaged in smuggling activities with the nearby village of Mudeford.

Fireworks by the Avon

Yachts moored on the Avon beneath the priory

# TUCKTONIA

On the road from Christchurch to Bournemouth, where a former toll bridge crosses the Stour, is Tucktonia — a place unique among holiday attractions. What started as a small complex of models of London landmarks, to a scale of 1:24, has grown into a four-acre site containing 200 sophisticated pieces by leading model makers, of places as varied as Stonehenge and a South Wales oil refinery.

In the London section, arranged along the banks of the Thames, are the Post Office Tower, standing 26 feet tall, and St Paul's at 14 feet. Tower Bridge and Big Ben are depicted, while the model of old London Bridge of 1624, which supported a small town, provides a marked contrast.

Christchurch Priory, Castle and Constable's House are featured, as well as a Cornish fishing village and the liner Queen Elizabeth II.

A stretch of motorway has been modelled, complete with its own miniature traffic, and there is a sophisticated computer-controlled model railway with nearly 200 items of rolling stock on a 2½ inch gauge track.

Tucktonia is claimed to be Europe's largest model landscape. Collectively the models depict not only Britain's historic past, her architecture, industry, and transport, but keep up to date with technological achievement. An oil rig and a nuclear power station are among the latest additions.

It is not a silent, inanimate collection of models. Trains and motor cars speed along the tracks and motorways, ships sail the seas, and planes taxi to take-off positions. Organ music greets you as you approach St Paul's Cathedral and Big Ben chimes the hours in this unbelieveable Britain in miniature, all created on the banks of the Dorset river Stour.

Tucktonia also has a large amusement park with a pitch and putt course, and cafeteria facilities.

# CHRISTCHURCH MUSEUM

One product of the region was finely worked 'fusee' chain used in clockmaking. Its manufacture was a cottage industry which became one of the occupations of the residents in the workhouse. Some of their efforts are on display, as well as household goods, tools and toys of the period. A large fireplace is used as a background for the old iron equipment for boiling and roasting in the days before kitchen ranges were available.

A natural history gallery shows the richness and variety of the area around Christchurch and the Hengistbury Head. Birds, animals and vegetation are depicted in lifelike dioramas, matched with photographs.

The garden of the Red House Museum

Open throughout the year, Tue - Sat all day, Sun afternoons
Price guide B

Inside the museum

The Red House Museum was bequeathed by the Druitt family who have been dedicated to creating a museum at Christchurch since Victorian times. The collection is regional and records domestic life as well as local industrial activities and geology. There is also a room devoted to the different prehistoric cultures of Wessex up to Roman times, and flints, axes, pottery and burial remains are on display.

The museum building, owned by the family, has a fascinating history. It was built near the priory in 1767 as a parish workhouse by the churchwardens and overseers of the poor, in trust for the parishioners, for the 'more comfortable support of their numerous poor'. One hundred and and thirty people were accommodated at a cost of six modern pence a head, per week.

With two major southern rivers on its doorstep — the Dorset Stour, a coarse fishing stream, and the Hampshire Avon, well known for its salmon — it is natural that the museum should have an aquarium, which although small has several examples of freshwater fish.

The grounds of the old workhouse have been turned into a beautiful old-world garden, and there is also an art gallery which features local artists' work.

The museum is literally in the shadow of the priory on the road which leads from the bottom of the High Street to the Quay, and is only a few minutes walk from the buses which come from Bournemouth. A free leaflet guide to a local walk around many of the historical features of the town is available from the museum sales desk.

The front of the old workhouse building

# MUDEFORD

The cottages on the quay

Low tide at Mudeford

At the seaward end of the Stanpit Marshes, which form a large part of Christchurch Harbour, the fishing village of Mudeford hugs the shore. It takes its name from the little river Mude which joins the Stour and the Avon within the harbour.

Although now almost surrounded by modern development, the original village is an attractive mixture of Georgian and Victorian homes, and includes a row of quaint Dutch-style cottages and an ancient inn, built on a sandspit by the entrance to Christchurch Harbour. At the Avon beach is a strange house called Gundimore, built in the late 18th century in the shape of a Persian tent. Its original owner, William Stuart Rose, was apparently a lover of camping. Among the friends who visited him there were Coleridge, Southey, and Sir Walter Scott. The latter revised his *Marmion* while staying there in 1807.

Both George III and Squire Tregonwell, the founder of modern Bournemouth, visited Mudeford. This encouraged the locals to hope that it would become a popular resort. It was not to be. The King went on to Weymouth, and Tregonwell transferred his attentions further down the coast.

Mudeford found another source of wealth, however. The channel into Christchurch Harbour, known as the Run, became a notorious landing place for smugglers, and many residents of the district made fortunes and then became respected citizens. The 18th and 19th century smugglers dealt with goods such as spirits, tea, lace, raisins, playing cards and tobacco. Simple commodities, unlike today's drug trading.

The Government, in an attempt to stamp out the smuggling, stepped up their precautions between Swanage and Southampton, yet the comings and goings of these 'Gentlemen of the Night' were common knowledge in Christchurch and Mudeford. Even schoolboys used to cheer when they saw the smuggler Slippery Rogers sail down the estuary.

On the 15th July 1784, a famous battle was fought at Mudeford, in a confrontation between smugglers and the Royal Navy. Excise men had helplessly watched as smugglers unloaded two luggers full of tea and spirits in broad daylight, and saucily used 50 wagons and 400 horses to move the cargo.

Next day, the 100-foot sloop of war *Orestes*, with 18 guns, arrived to help the two revenue cutters. When the navy men rowed ashore, the smugglers opened fire from their craft and from the shore, and sailing master William Allen was mortally wounded.

The smugglers eventually retreated and their boats were taken, but when the *Orestes* and the customs boats *Swan* and *Excise* left next day the authorities had little to be pleased about. Not one smuggler had been captured and none of the contraband was recovered. They say much of it found its way into Christchurch homes. The Ship in Distress Inn at Stanpit was a popular meeting place for the smugglers.

Today yachts and pleasure craft make more peaceful arrivals and departures through the Run, and ferry boats carry summer visitors to the sandy beaches on the Hengistbury shore. During the season, from February to the end of July, fishermen can be watched while they catch the famous Christchurch salmon in the Run, using seine nets. A small shop for the sale of seafood is a popular attraction on the spit.

# HENGISTBURY HEAD

From Mudeford, a little ferry fussing across the strongly flowing current of the Run — the channel into Christchurch Harbour — brings the explorer to Hengistbury Head, one of the few places of real antiquity on the Bournemouth scene.

Situated at the eastern end of Bournemouth's seven miles of sand and pebble beach, it stands like a sentinel. At its highest point, it offers a splendid viewpoint for the Avon and Stour valleys, Christchurch harbour, the Isle of Wight and Bournemouth.

Most visitors approach Hengistbury Head from Bournemouth. Buses run right up to the Double Dykes where the ancient earth fortifications stretch from the sea across to Christchurch Harbour, forming a landward defence to the headland which is otherwise surrounded by water. The Dykes, which were built in the Iron Age, now only protect a great expanse of grass which suddenly rises up to the summit 180 feet high. On the seaward side there is a sheer cliff face to the beach.

Although this ia favourite picnic area, visitors are requested to keep to the paths when climbing the slopes to avoid further erosion.

Before the Romans arrived in Britain, there was a British mint below the hill, and relics and coins have been found.

In the Napoleonic Wars, a battery was established on the highest point of the head because it was believed that the Emperor would attempt to land his forces along the sandy coast between Hengistbury and Poole. At Trafalgar, Nelson destroyed Napoleon's fleet and his dream, and the battery was never needed.

The view from the hilltop, across the placid estuary of the Avon and Stour, encompasses the Stanpit Marshes — an established bird sanctuary. Beyond the dominant Christchurch Priory tower is the hill of St Catherine, on which it was originally intended to build the Priory (see Christchurch). If you turn to the west you can enjoy the expanse of yellow cliffs and sands extending past Bournemouth to Sandbanks.

Hengistbury Head is the site of the magnificent new headquarters for the coastguards which gives them a panoramic view of the Poole Bay, the Needles channel and Solent approaches. A short walk westward are the deep excavations made to extract ironstone, which now form a picturesque hilltop lake. The ironstone was formerly conveyed by barges from the harbour below to Bucklers Hard, where it was smelted into iron for shipbuilding. Some of that iron found its way into the fine ships of Nelson's Navy.

The lakeside is a viewpoint for the Mudeford Harbour entrance and the famous Christchurch salmon run. Beyond are the muddy cliffs of Highcliffe, Barton on Sea and Hurst Castle. After descending through the excavated area, the explorer will reach the harbour shore From the beach hut settlement, he can walk back through the thick woodland or travel on the little trackless 'Noddy' train, which runs a continuous service from Double Dykes.

# BOURNEMOUTH

This perfumed resort of fragrant pines is unique among British seaside towns. Less than 200 years ago, the land on which Bournemouth now stands was a sandy moorland.

In 1796, when Europe was dominated by Napoleon, a Captain Lewis Tregonwell was in charge of a troop of the Dorset Yeomanry patrolling the seven miles of coast at Bournemouth. Some years later, in 1810, while holidaying with his rich wife at Mudeford, he drove her to the area. They liked it so much that he bought land, and built his house on the site of what is now the Royal Exeter Hotel near the Square.

It was Tregonwell who planted the pine trees in the deep romantic chines which nature cut into the seven miles of cliffs backing the golden sands. In Victorian days there were many sanatoriums in the town because the pine-scented air was supposed to be a cure for tuberculosis. Many visitors came for rest cures, and were pulled around the town in elegant bathchairs.

Although the town was so recently established, there is evidence that Neolithic men lived on the site. The skull of the 'Bournemouth Man' was unearthed at Longham in 1932 and was thought to be 5,500 years old; even earlier remains, of a camp of the Palaeolithic period, have been found on Warren Hill at Hengistbury Head. These have been dated to about 10,000 BC.

The Pleasure Gardens by night

At Bournemouth the cliffs dip to form a wide valley which allows the Bourne stream to enter the sea. From this point, the Pleasure Gardens have been established along the banks of the stream right up to the Poole boundary two miles away.

A quarter of a mile inland, the Bourne is conduited under the Square, the hub of the shopping centre for which Bournemouth is well known. Between the Square and the sea, the gardens have been developed into lawns — an auditorium for those who come to hear the bands which play in the Pine Walk bandstand. They are perfectly laid out with flower beds and blossoming cherry trees, making it difficult to believe that cattle grazed on the site before the turn of the century.

All roads into town converge on the Square like spokes into a wheel hub. Beyond this busy centre, the gardens encompass the War Memorial and pass the great Victorian hotel, which is now the Town Hall. From there onwards, the gardens slowly become wilder in character until tall poplar trees line the river banks, and noisy little waterfalls splash over the weirs. This is the town's most beautiful walk, all the way to the Poole boundary without leaving the gardens.

Bournemouth ranks among the leading resorts in the world. It is a sophisticated retreat which still maintains much of the exclusive upper-class atmosphere on which it built its reputation.

Westbourne remembers Robert Louis Stevenson. His home, Skerryvore, at the top of Alum Chine, was bombed during the last war and the foundation outline forms the centrepiece of a memorial garden. He lived here in poor health for three years and wrote *Kidnapped* and *Dr Jekyll and Mr Hyde*. The son of the poet Shelley lived in Boscombe, and a private theatre at his home Boscombe Manor (now Shelley Park) is being restored.

Lily Langtry's house

Shelley's grave

Shelley's heart lies in a vault in the shadow of St Peter's, the parish church designed by George Edmund Street R.A. in 1879. The hymn writer John Keble is also buried there, while at rest in the Wimborne Road cemetery is Canon Twells whose lovely hymn *At even, ere the sun was set*, is sung all over the world.

The parish church has a central position in the town, highlighting the leading role established religion played in Victorian Bournemouth. The town was also a Non-Conformist stronghold. The noted Free Church leader, Dr J.D. Jones, orated from Richmond Hill Congregational Church for nearly 40 years. A keen cricketer and follower of Hampshire, it is said that he mistakenly uttered 'Over', instead of 'Amen' at a service during a cricket festival. In 1906, General Bramwell Booth preached a sermon from an open touring car in Bournemouth Square.

Gladstone uttered his last public speech at Central Station. He was going home to die and there was a crowd gathered on the platform. 'God bless you sir', someone called. Gladstone slowly turned and raised his hat. 'God bless you all, this place, and the land we love', he replied. It was 1898 when oratory was a cherished In 1898 oratory was a cherished attribute.

Those who thrill to a little romance will want to see the love nest where Lillie Langtry lived and entertained King Edward VII, in Derby road off the main Christchurch road. It is now a hotel bearing her name. You can dine there and see the minstrels' gallery and the King's peephole on the first floor. If you are lucky you may stay in his bedroom, now restored with its original decoration and inglenook.

Winston Churchill came as a little boy to sail his toy yacht in Bourne stream. In the 1980s, children still do.

At Southbourne, near Hengistbury Head, there is a plaque which marks the spot where Charles Stuart Rolls of Rolls-Royce fame, a pioneer aviator, was killed during an air show in 1910.

In spite of its short history, Bournemouth has an abundance of museums for the explorer to visit after he has wandered in the lush parks, colourful gardens, countless bowling greens and three first-class golf courses. The town has also become established as a casino centre.

The mammoth British International Centre (BIC) opened in 1984 in Exeter road near the pier. It not only caters for major conferences but houses restaurants, bars, a concert hall and even a swimming pool with artificially-made waves.

The British International Centre

# WINE & DINE IN A TRANQUIL RIVERSIDE SETTING

FRESH FOOD · FRIENDLY SERVICE · A RELAXING
ATMOSPHERE · THE BRIDGE HOUSE · A PLEASURE TO VISIT

The Bridge House offers luxurious hotel
accommodation and a wonderful relaxed
atmosphere for wining and dining, only a
short drive from Bournemouth.

**BARS & HOT CARVERY**
on the ground floor.
Extensive riverside bars, with real ale, fine
wines, carvery – prices to suit all tastes

**ANNA'S RESTAURANT**
on the first floor.
Outstanding English and Continental
Cuisine. Fresh food, excellent service, Music
and Dancing.

**LUXURIOUS ACCOMMODATION**
30 beautifully appointed bedrooms with
private facilities. Business, Holidays, Bargain
Breaks.

The Bridge House for Morning Coffee,
Afternoon Cream Teas. Extensive Free
Parking. Facilities for Children.

# THE BRIDGE HOUSE
## HOTEL · FREE HOUSE
2 RINGWOOD ROAD, LONGHAM · TEL. BOURNEMOUTH (0202) 578828

# BOURNEMOUTH MUSEUMS

Sir Merton Russell Cotes, one of Bournemouth's most public-spirited citizens, gave his home on the East Cliff for use as a museum and art gallery. The unique 1894 building perched on the east cliffside was bequeathed complete with all the treasures collected on his world travels. It is museum of the 'old school', where you whisper as you descend the great staircase lest the weapons and native implements fall off the walls. There are porcelains of many periods, precious items, miniatures and enamels; furniture of English, Dutch and French origin; Japanese and Burmese treasures; cases of butterflies; autographed letters by Sir Walter Scott, Garibaldi, Ruskin and Florence Nightingale and a lock of Nelson's hair, cut off a week before he died.

The suite of art galleries was added in 1919 and 1926, and contains works by the best-known artists of the 19th and 20th century. The Irving Room contains some of Sir Henry Irving's costumes, together with jewels and many relics and portraits of the famous actor.

One of the most unusual objects in the museum is the last Bournemouth bathchair. After a previous curator refused to find room for it in the 1960s, the author was pulled around town in the chair to stir up public interest. It now has a place of honour.

A freshwater aquarium, stocked with fish from local rivers, has been opened adjacent to the museum tea rooms.

Also to be seen in the museum is the Lucas collection of old English oak furniture, and the Meader collection of Victoriana, armour and firearms. It contains butterflies and moths from all over the world, and a fantastic collection of sea-shells and sea-bed specimens. Modern revolvers and duelling pistols jostle with spectacles, jewellery, cuff links, collar studs and hat pins, and a Maori war canoe. Believe it or not, there is also a cloak made from peacock and pigeon feathers.

The Casa Magni Shelley Museum is at Shelley Park, Beechwood Avenue, Boscombe, and is unique in being the only museum devoted solely to the poet Percy Bysshe Shelley. The house was originally called Boscombe Manor, and was the home of the poet's son, Sir Percy Florence Shelley, from 1849 to 1889. The museum takes its name from Casa Magni in Italy, Shelley's last place of residence. It was there that the collection had its first home, being opened on the 150th anniversary of the poet's death in 1972. Bournemouth Council offered the collection a new home when the house in Italy was sold. It has been here since 1979.

Bournemouth Transport Museum is at the Mallard Road bus depot off Castle Lane in Bournemouth's outskirts. Transport enthusiasts help in this venture, in collaboration with Bournemouth Museums. The exhibition is open in the summer, and visitors can see tramcar No. 85 (1914) — one of the original Bournemouth trams which journeyed from Poole to Christchurch. It is restored to all its former grandeur and livery. Other vehicles include an open-top bus and a trolley-bus and most of the different buses used in Bournemouth to transport visitors and residents over the last 60-odd years. School parties requiring a guide or lecture should apply through the curator of Bournemouth Museums.

The Mobile Museum is a former corporation bus built by Leyland in 1960. When it was withdrawn from service in 1976, it was one of the last of the traditional two-doorway, two-staircase vehicles. Converted, it now carries a series of interchangeable exhibitions which are taken to towns and villages in the area.

The Russell Cotes Museum, built in 1894

The Big Four Railway Museum and Model Centre is a private exhibition at Dalkeith Steps, 81b Old Christchurch Road, near Beales' store. It features 2000 railway relics and has a working model railway.

For the serious minded the private Bournemouth Natural Science Museum is at 39 Old Christchurch Road. It welcomes visitors, but visits must be booked in advance by writing to the Hon. Secretary, c/o the Museum. It is free, and features exhibits on archaeology, ancient Egyptian mammals, entomology, botany, ornithology, astronomy, and geography. There is an excellent diorama showing the animals which can be seen in the New Forest.

The Victorian interior of the Russell Cotes Museum

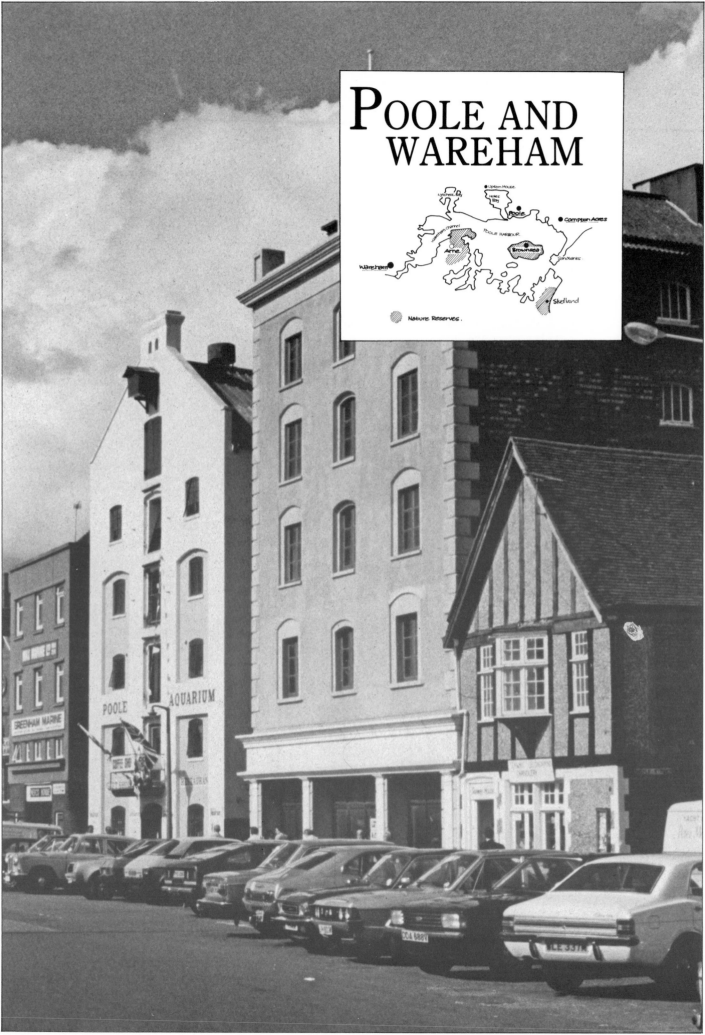

# POOLE AND WAREHAM

# NEW POOLE

The Poole Authorities were heavily criticised when they bulldozed much of old Poole in the 1940s, but it was a merciful release for some of those who lived in the decaying properties, in lanes so narrow that their only daylight was reflected off whitewashed walls. The old port, with its dowdy one-street shopping centre, was boldly transformed into a town which now presents itself with pride as a leading leisure resort. At the same time, the commercial port entered a new period of prosperity, with the development of the roll-on-roll-off ferry terminal. Factory estates grew up on the outskirts and, by the middle 1980s, Poole had become the fastest-growing town in England with a population of over 100,000.

The most important redevelopment was at the top of the town where the High Street met the Bournemouth and Wimborne roads in a great square. All the buildings disappeared, including a theatre, except the George Hotel. This now stands amid a vast complex of modern architecture, including the massive Barclays International building and the enormous enclosed Arndale shopping precinct, which — at one point — is built on the old High Street. Here also is the Arts Centre, housing a theatre, concert hall, cinema and conference suites: a building that the authorities are justifiably proud of.

A stylish flyover bridge now takes the traffic to the harbour and Hamworthy, avoiding long waits at the train gates where the railway runs through the heart of Poole.

Poole is some distance from her lovely sandy pleasure beaches at Branksome and Sandbanks, but they can be easily reached by road. Buses run from Poole town centre, and from Bournemouth. Some of the harbour shallows have been reclaimed to make parks; the largest, Poole Park, uses the Weymouth - London railway as a boundary in the harbour, and it forms a large shallow lake with lawns around it where youngsters can hire boats and sail and row in safety. There are bowling greens and tennis courts, as well as a model railway, all within a few minutes' walking distance from the town centre.

The Arndale Centre (left) and the Barclays International building

Poole's modern Civic Centre is adjacent to the park, and is well worth a visit. Council offices, social services, police HQ and law courts form a neat island complex, and the very new hospital dominates the skyline behind the park.

Whitecliff is another, smaller reclamation on the shore of Parkstone Bay, and can be reached from Poole Park via a tunnel under the railway. This park, which has a cricket pitch, is adjacent to the most recent and controversial harbour reclamation, Baiter Point. Situated between Poole Park and Fishermans Dock at Poole Quay, the park was once a sandy peninsular, with a fever hospital at the point. Beneath the grass of this popular playground lie the bones of some of those who died of the plague in the 15th century.

Modern Poole Quay has adapted many of its picturesque warehouses to house clubs, restaurants and even an aquarium, and a visit to Poole Potteries is a must. Explorers can come and watch the potters at work and purchase their famous wares. There are also some fine old inns, where you will rub shoulders with the crews of some of the ships docked in the port.

Across the Town Bridge Hamworthy, the new commercial port, has been built on reclaimed land and the visitor will see that a special harbour has been built for the Poole Yacht Club's exclusive use.

The overbearing power station at Hamworthy, built in 1950, gives low-lying Poole its one dominating vertical feature. It forms a background to the harbour activities, behind the Hamworthy bridge, a massive cube of yellow brick with two lofty chimneys which serve as landmarks for yachtsmen and fishermen out in the bay.

The lake at Poole Park

**MUSEUMS** The local and maritime history of Poole. Located in three superb sites in the Old Town within easy reach of each other. TAKE A STEP INTO THE PAST at:
*Guildhall Museum, Market Street, Old Town.*
*The Maritime Museum, Town Cellars.*
*Scaplen's Court Museum, High Street.*

**POOLE AQUARIUM AND SERPENTARIUM**
Take lunch with a crocodile or tea with a shark. Get as close to a piranha as you would ever dare. Together with poisonous snakes and a bird-eating spider, these are just some of the attractions to be found in this fascinating collection. Fun for all the family.
*Poole Quay, Poole.*

**MERLEY BIRD GARDENS**
The perfect place for a family day out. Exotic and brilliant birds, a pet shop, play and picnic areas with free parking. Plus the superb Orangery Restaurant. All this just off the A31 Wimborne by-pass.
*Merley, Nr. Wimborne, Dorset.*

**COMPTON ACRES**
Without question, some of the finest gardens in Europe. Open from April 1st to the end of October, from 10.30 a.m. till 6.30 p.m. every day including Sundays. Everything from a semi-tropical glen to the beautiful, formal Roman and Italian gardens. Refreshments available.
*Canford Cliffs, Poole, Dorset.*

**J. BOLSONS & SON LTD**
Fascinating boat trips from both Poole and Bournemouth. Cruise in comfort to the Isle of Wight or enjoy the harbour and islands of Poole. Take an evening cruise to sample the beauty of this stretch of the Purbeck coast. Our boats are also available for private parties and functions.
*Booking offices: Tourist Information Office, Poole Quay. Tel: 673322 or Pier Approach, Bournemouth. Tel: 28550.*

**HARVEYS PLEASURE BOATS**
Ferry services, trips and harbour cruises. A unique way to see the full, breathtaking beauty of this magnificent harbour, its islands lakelands and the surrounding Purbeck Hills Picnic on Brownsea Island with red squirrels or journey to the Roman town of Wareham Regular sailings, see our timetable.
*Fish Shambles Steps, Poole Quay.*

**THE DOLPHIN SWIMMING POOL**
Get your family in the swim. From babies to proficient swimmers, all are catered for. With a sauna, sun terrace and refreshment area to provide a complete family outing.
*Kingland Road, Poole, Dorset.*

**SPORTS CENTRE**
Superb indoor sports facilities for squash, badminton, table tennis, Judo and Karate, five-a-side football and volleyball. Holidaymakers are welcome to play or watch. Open 7 days a week from 9 a.m. to 11 p.m. With pleasant bar and refreshment facilities.
*The Arndale Shopping Centre, 2nd Floor.*

**ARTS CENTRE**
Arts, exhibitions and entertainments in one superb Centre. The Wessex Hall, Towngate Theatre, Ashley Cinema and Seldown Gallery provide superior venues for a wide range of activities. The real pleasure of leisure with restaurants and bars throughout the Centre.
*Kingland Road, Poole.*

**TOURISM CENTRE**
Poole's Information Centre on the Quay. Everything you want to know about what you can do or see in Poole and the surrounding area. An absolute must for planning your holiday here. Including a computerised vacancy finding service. Our friendly staff are always ready to answer your questions, and show you our own range of souvenir posters, books, postcards, pottery and craft items.
*The Quay, Poole.*

# Poole... centre of activity

# OLD POOLE

Most of old Poole can be explored during a short walk along the harbour front, with its colourful frontage of 18th-century warehouses and seamen's inns blending with edifices of more modern times. The route weaves in and out of little streets with lovely names like Old Orchard, Sarum and Paradise. To fully enjoy the perambulation, however, it is well to know a little of Poole's past.

The town stands on a peninsular within the great harbour, flanked by Holes Bay and Parkstone Bay. Men of the Old and New Stone Age lived on the site, and burial places dating from the Bronze and Iron Ages have been excavated. It was an important base for the Romans, but they built their commercial port on the other shore of Holes Bay, at Hamworthy.

The town was pillaged and burnt by marauders on countless occasions. When Canute invaded England in 1015 it was at Poole he landed, and the cry around the street 'The Danes, the Danes are coming!' must have struck terror into the hearts of the early townspeople.

By the end of the 12th century silting in the Wareham Channel, and the fact that the ships were becoming larger, necessitated the building of an important port nearer the sea. This marked the beginning of Poole's prosperity and the decline of Wareham, and started a long feud between the towns.

The Fisheries Office (left) and the Custom House

The Longespee Charter of 1248 partly separated Poole from the Manor of Canford, indicating that it was becoming a busy trading centre. In 1433, Henry VI made the town a Port of Staple; this allowed it to import and export wool, woollen cloth, leather and metal, and the 15th and 16th centuries were, therefore, times of great prosperity.

With the growth of trade with Newfoundland, in fish and their associated products, Poole had a second flush of prosperity in the 17th century. European countries, short of food, were glad to accept the dried cod which the Poole merchants sold at high prices. The merchants returned to England with wine, which being in short supply here fetched a good price in London. The resulting influx of wealth encouraged extensive building in the port which continued into the 18th century, and the architecture of this period still dominates the old town today.

By the beginning of the 19th century, Poole had amassed a fleet of nearly 300 ships, 80 of which were engaged in the Newfoundland trade. The harbour sometimes resembled a forest of leafless trees with the tall masts dominating the skyline.

Some of the flavour of bygone days can be savoured in the Old Town as it is today. Walk from the Town Bridge along the Quay until you reach the Custom House, with its pair of curved steps leading to a porch with Tuscan columns. Built in 1788, it was reconstructed after a fire in 1813. You are now standing in a preserved part of Old Poole. On the left is the old Harbour Office of 1822, now used by H.M. Customs, with its open lower storey and Tuscan columns, while on the right in Paradise Street are the Old Town Cellars, a 15th-century stone building which is now a museum.

A cargo ship loading at Poole

The tower of the parish church of St James is visible in the background. This church was rebuilt in 1820 and is the centrepiece of another part of the port which has been preserved around Thames Street. Two of the residences here display the opulence of the town's shipping merchants: the Mansion House of 1790 and Poole House, with its brick parapet decorated with urns. There are several such mansions around the town, but Poole's most famous private house is Scaplen's Court, at the bottom of the High Street, a 14th and 15th-century house (see Poole Museums).

Near the church in St Clement's Lane is a portion of the old town wall. Richard III promised not only to build a town wall, but also a gateway to the port. He did not keep his promise, and the surviving fragment was probably paid for by the town. Looking along Church Street and its continuation, Market Street, gives a good idea of old Poole. The Guildhall dominates the top of the street. The St George's Almshouses are comparatively modern — the plaque is dated 1904 — but the original almshouses they replaced were built in the time of Henry V. They passed to the Crown in 1547, and were purchased by Poole Corporation in 1550. They have provided homes for the poor for 500 years.

The explorer interested in the merchants' residences will love West End House near St James Church, Joliffe House in West Quay road, Beech Hurst in the High Street, and Sir Peter Thompson's house in Market Close. All are gems in their own way. Beech Hurst, built in 1783, is set back above the main street by a flight of steps to a semicircular porch with Tuscan columns. Three storeys of red brick are topped by a pediment containing a shield of arms, embraced by palm fronds. West End House, built in 1716, features a parapet balustraded with pineapples and heavy urns.

At the end of the Town Quay is the Fisherman's Dock, a harbour enclosed behind a breakwater, with an old lifeboat station complete with disused lifeboat. Here on the quay wall the old salts sit and talk as they mend their nets, as their predecessors have done for centuries before them.

The Old Town and harbour

# Shop in comfort whatever the weather

Easy to find, easy to park and easy to stay, the Arndale Centre in the heart of Poole has **around 100 shops all under its one roof!**

Boots, Littlewoods, Beales, Marks & Spencer, Mothercare, Richards, Dorothy Perkins, Dixons, Burtons, Menzies, Toy Shops, Apollo, food shops, & independent specialist shops plus more.

| Car Parking | Bus Terminus | Safe for the Kids | Sports Facilities | Library |
|---|---|---|---|---|

# POOLE MUSEUMS

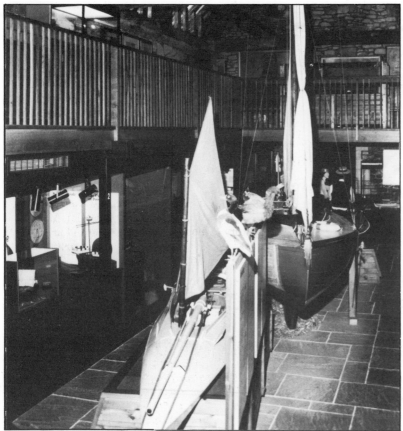

The Maritime Museum in the Town Cellars

Guildhall, Scaplen's Court and Maritime Museums open:
Mon-Sat 10.00-5.00
Sun 2.00-5.00
Price guide A (each)
B (all 3)
Lifeboat Museum open Mon-Fri 9.30 - 4.30

Figureheads in the Maritime Museum

The buildings which form Poole's three museums are as exciting as the exhibits they contain, a credit to the town's enthusiastic young curator Graham Smith M.A., A.D.F.

The Maritime Museum was formerly the Town Cellars, a mainly 15th-century building situated on the quayside. When it was built the harbour wall was much further back, and the area around has been the focal point of the port's activities for many centuries.

Before its conversion in the 1970s, this portion of the Town Cellars was the subject of a major archaeological excavation during which the whole of the interior was probed. It was found that during the 18th and 19th centuries the building was used mainly for storage of maritime goods. The 'occupation debris' was punctuated by several floor levels, which continued down in an irregular fashion giving consistent evidence that the structure had always been used for industrial and commercial purposes. A floor level relating to the 17th century produced a number of finely constructed hearths used for industrial purposes, each about 20 inches in diameter. The earliest layers, which related to the 13th century, were some five feet below the present level and it was decided to retain this level for the main floor of the museum.

Detailed architectural examination of the structure suggests that the building is probably of two phases, the earliest being late 13th. In the 15th century substantial alterations were made, including the complete rebuilding of the south wall. This rebuilding could possibly be associated with Poole's rise in status during this period. In 1512, a document refers to it as a woolhouse, obviously a store for the main commodity of the Staple: woollen goods brought in from the Dorset sheep-rearing areas.

The museum today has two full size local craft. The prototype 'X' class racing keel boat has a place of honour. It was designed by Alfred Westmacott in 1908 as a sailing boat for the Royal Motor Yacht Club. So magnificent and far-sighted was his yacht that the class is still sailed extensively along the coast, with a major fleet at Poole. X1 *Grebe*, formerly *Mistletoe*, with its mast stepped, just clears the 15th-century beams by six inches. The other craft in the museum is a Poole wildfowling punt and gun of 1901 vintage.

The local development of the port is also portrayed, and there are items belonging to Sir Ernest Shackleton, and artefacts from the ship *Pandora* concerned in the mutiny on the *Bounty*.

Scaplen's Court is the best preserved and most complete domestic building of the late medieval period existing in the town. It was described by the Chief Inspector of Ancient Monuments, on the occasion of his visit of inspection in 1950, as 'one of the finest examples of a 15th-century town house on the south coast'.

Scaplen's Court

It has been suggested that Scaplen's Court was the building referred to when John Leland, the eminent Tudor antiquary, visited Poole during Henry VIII's reign between the years 1536 and 1542 and noted, among other buildings of interest, a 'fair town house of stone by the kay'. There is certainly a possibility that Leland was referring to Scaplen's Court because the buildings of the south wing with their sixty-foot frontage on the 'Great Quays' must have constituted a 'fair town house'.

The kitchen at Scaplen's Court, and the roof timbering

For about 150 years the upper story also served as the venue for Poole Quarter Sessions, the Magistrates' Court and the Poole Court of Admiralty. The southern courts seemed very fond of transporting criminals as a punishment. In 1764, Constant Savage was convicted of felony and transported to one of His Majesty's colonies or plantations in America for the term of seven years. Today she would probably have been placed on probation. There were many smugglers tried in the old Guildhall, and the visitors sitting quietly among today's museum exhibits can chuckle when they think of James Bugden who, in 1853, was fined one shilling for 'using a cart drawn by dogs'. The arcaded — and now glassed in — ground floor of the building, the 'shambles', consisted of ten open-fronted shops until about 1850. On the roof there is a square lantern, surmounted by a cornice and octagonal dome with a weather vane.

The whole building is now a museum with displays of civic charters and scenes depicting the growth of Poole. There is a section for temporary exhibitions and — a modern touch in this ancient place — an audio-visual display which depicts Poole life in pictures.

When the Royal National Lifeboat Institution moved its headquarters to West Quay Road in Poole and set up their repair yard on the harbour shore, another Poole museum was founded.

Within the RNLI headquarters is the small Lifeboat Museum, which traces the 160-year-old history and development of the RNLI through lifeboat models, paintings, photographs, commemorative items and insignia. The largest exhibit is a fully-equipped inshore lifeboat.

The museum tries to convey the fine traditions of the service — its skilled volunteer crew members and the support of hundreds of dedicated fundraisers — and its modern and highly efficient approach to the ever-increasing demands of the service. (In 1983 lifeboats were launched an average of ten times each day, and saved more than three lives each day.)

As the permanent secretariat for the International Lifeboat Conference, of which there are over thirty member countries including the Soviet Union, China, Japan and the USA, the RNLI receives many overseas visitors and a small part of the museum is devoted to a demonstration of this international co-operation.

The Society of Poole Men were instrumental in saving this historic place. During restoration work in 1923 a chimney collapsed causing damage which enabled the local historian, H.P. Smith, to make the discoveries which proved that it was substantially a late medieval building. In another gale in 1925, a further fall of masonry caused the restoration project to be temporarily abandoned.

In 1927 the Society, at the wish of Mr Smith, raised funds for a second attempt at restoration, and the building was eventually opened to the public in 1929. Closed again in 1950 because it was found unsound, gradual renovation work was carried out and it was re-opened by Poole Corporation in 1959.

Scaplen's Court has two storeys with a cellar, walls of coursed rubble and later brickwork, and roofs covered with tiles and stone slates. The building is basically of Purbeck stone with some dressings of Bath Stone, but many cobbles are incorporated which are not of local origin and may have been brought to Poole as ship's ballast. The structure comprises four ranges set around a rectangular courtyard. The ranges to the south-east and south-west appear to have been built first, but these were closely followed by the other ranges enclosing the courtyard.

The building houses 'domestic living' displays of the 19th and early 20th centuries, with an archaeological display upstairs.

The Old Guildhall in Market Street, built in 1761, was the gift of the town's MPs. Like the Custom House on the Quay, it has two semicircular flights of steps to a big Tuscan porch. This was the entrance to the Guildhall, which served as such until the opening of the new Municipal Buildings at Park Gates in 1932.

The Guildhall Museum

# COMPTON ACRES

Open daily 1 April - 31 Oct
10.30 - 6.00 (or until dusk
on Thursdays in June,
July and August)

It seems to have become a habit in Dorset for men to create beauty out of savage moorland. Tregonwell built his Bournemouth around the coastal heaths, and on the slopes that overlook Poole Harbour at Canford Cliffs, Thomas William Simpson bought a 1914-built house after the First World War, and laid out a series of beautiful gardens, each designed so that only one garden could be seen at a time. Out of the wilderness of golden gorse, purple heather, Scots pine and windswept bushes, on slopes of yellow sand, he created ten gardens which are unique in this country, to which visitors by the thousand have come — like pilgrims — for nearly 70 years.

The inspired planning and construction took several years and cost about £220,000. Thousands of tons of stone and good topsoil were brought from far and wide. For the Japanese garden, a whole shipload of flowers and plants and bushes were brought to Poole from the East, and the Japanese gardeners came with them to lay it out. Bronze and marble statuary, lead figures and vases, fountains, wellheads and stone benches — many are museum pieces — were collected from many parts of the world.

What you will see today is not quite as Simpson planned, because the saga of Compton Acres concerns two more owners who have devoted time, money and love to maintain this beautiful place. Middleton, the famous head gardener at Compton Acres, died during the Second World War, and at the cessation of hostilities, when work could have started on renovating the gardens, the owner and genius who had created them also passed away. An inadequate staff tried to cope but nature was too strong for them. Trees merged overhead and the rhododendron banks became an almost impenetrable jungle. Less sun got through to the flowers, and even the birds began to desert.

In 1950 Mr Stanley Beard, an architect, bought the property, restored it and once more opened the gardens to the public. The decaying peat banks were replaced by walls of beautiful Purbeck stone, and alternative paths were constructed to assist the elderly and mothers with prams. To put the project on a more secure financial basis, coach and car parks were built into the site. The present owners, John Brady and his wife, took over in 1964.

The flowers, trees and shrubs can be seen in various states through most of the year, for the gardens are open every day from April to the end of October.

The set tour leads from the enclosed circular Roman garden, through the herbacious borders to the famous and elegant Italian garden with its fountains and goldfish pond. The Palm Court features fine statuary, while the wilder woodland glen leads to a traditional English garden, with billiard-table lawns, flower borders and views of Poole Harbour and Brownsea Island.

The Garden of Memory was designed by Stanley Beard as a memorial to his son Dick, killed while serving in the RAF during the last war, and to his two daughters Elizabeth and Anne, both victims of polio.

In spite of all the variety of beauty, it is probably the Japanese garden which is most interesting — in fact it is believed to be the only one in Europe. As water cascades over the falls, you will meet the God of Punishment and, across a bowed bridge, arrive at the Imperial Tea House. The visitor leaves this strange garden with reluctance, because it really is something out of this world.

# POOLE HARBOUR

Green Island (foreground), Furzey Island and Brownsea, with Sandbanks behind

Where do you begin to explore this magnificent wild estuary, which lies like a lake, dotted with islands, beneath the glowering Purbeck Hills?. Perhaps you should go to Evening Hill between Sandbanks and Lilliput at sundown, following the example of that great painter J.M.W. Turner, who was inspired by the sunsets over the harbour. From this vantage point you have a superb view over one of the largest natural harbours in the world — 28 square miles of water with 90 miles of coastline, six bays and eight named islands. Fed by two Dorset rivers, the Frome and Piddle, and countless smaller ones descending from the Purbecks, it has only one seaward entry, a few hundred yards wide but 60 feet deep, scoured by the tides that race in and out. Across this deep gully runs the chain ferry, for the use of cars journeying to the Purbecks and Swanage.

A dug-out canoe dredged from the harbour bed was dated to 800 BC, and it is known that one of the oldest trading nations, the Phoenicians, visited Poole. The Romans used Poole and Hamworthy extensively from AD 43-450, and the builders of Hadrian's Wall received bulk supplies of pottery from Poole Harbour kilns.

Looking out from Evening Hill, the explorer can see the sweep of Whitley Lake to the left, in the corner of which is Poole's smallest and oldest yacht club, the East Dorset. The isthmus at Sandbanks with its single line of expensive properties is reflected in the placid water, and beyond is the rest of the Sandbanks and the jetties of the Royal Motor Yacht Club.

Brownsea is the nearest and biggest of the islands, masking Furzey Island and Green Island from view. The former may become a site for oil wells — to the disgust of lovers of the harbour, but Green Island is the home of a potter who lives a Robinson Crusoe-style of existence, making his exclusive pots from island clay and colouring them with minerals picked up on the shore. Long Island and Round Island are higher up the harbour, and there are some fine houses on the latter. Only Brownsea is open to the public.

Holes Bay is beyond the Poole Town Quay and bridge, and has the RNLI headquarters and yard and a large yachting complex on its shores. Here also is Cobbs Quay, one of the largest yacht marinas in the south of England. Between Evening Hill and the Town Quay is Parkstone Bay, which will probably be converted into a deep-water yacht haven. Parkstone and Poole Harbour Yacht Clubs are in this area, the latter having use of a large marina. There is a public launching slipway at Baiter Point, near the Fisherman's Dock.

Although the visitor can make contact with the harbour at several points, it is best explored by a boat trip from Poole Town Quay, or by the larger ships which sail from Bournemouth Pier and cruise around bays of the harbour — known as the Dorset Lakes.

X-class yachts racing in Poole Harbour

If the explorer has a shallow-draught cruiser, he can spend days sailing into creeks and bays all the way to Wareham, without leaving the confines of the harbour. Fishing trips can be booked at the harbour throughout the summer. Harvey's run boats to Brownsea Island and around the other islands, starting from Pottery Steps.

The principal commercial users of the port are Truckline cross-channel ferry boats, which make two or three trips a day from Hamworthy transporting massive lorries to and from countries all over Europe, via Cherbourg. A second bay for loading has been built to deal with the ever-increasing traffic. No passengers are carried, but the lorry drivers have luxury accommodation aboard in which to relax. This Hamworthy shore, long ago the port for invading Romans, has become busy and important in modern times. A large slipway serves the Royal Marine Training centre, and a holiday caravan camp surrounds a complex of swimming pool, restaurant, shops and bars, which are open to the public, at Rockley Point.

Poole docks

# The most interesting Pub in the South

Atmospherically the kind of pub you dream about. A thatched roof greeting and within a wealth of memorabilia, curios and keepsakes — so absorbing that one could forget to ask for the menu and that would be a pity. Choice of bar snacks or full course meals in the restaurant, and Sunday lunches are a treat — as good as Mum makes at home! Emphasis is on home-made fare utilising local produce and providing variety. Four kinds of Ploughman's, help-yourself salad, basket meals and four unusual sausage blendings. Grills are popular, as is the Carvery with its oven-cooked roasts. Dorset Apple Cake and cream, and ice creams with unusual flavours are among the desserts. Chosen as UK Pub of the Year 1983/84.

* 20th Century Statistics
* Stamps, coins, skittles
* Glass beehives, holograms and birds eggs.
* Value for money.
* Warm and friendly welcome.
* Good wholesome homemade food.

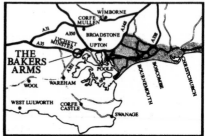

## THE BAKERS ARMS
LYTCHETT MINSTER, POOLE, DORSET. Tel: (0202) 622900

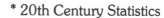

### Restaurant
Cocktail Bar Overlooking Poole Quay & Harbour
The finest local sea food & prime steaks
Open every day lunch & evening.
Credit cards & Business accounts welcome
**Reservations: Poole (0202) 674184**

### Corkers Wine Bar & Restaurant Poole Quay, Poole

### Wine Bar
* RELAIS ROUTIERS RECOMMENDED *
* Live Entertainment
* Extensive Wine List
* Superb Cold Buffet
Hot Food Menu at prices you can afford
**Telephone: Poole (0202) 681393**

# UPTON HOUSE PARK

Upton House Park, Poole's premier open space, now belongs to the town because of the generosity of the Llewellin family. It is maintained by the Council with the aid of the Friends of Upton Country Park.

Upton house from the south

The Friends were formed in 1976 as a charity to assist the Council in the restoration of the house and grounds, which had become an overgrown jungle. They created a car park and picnic area around the north front of the house, restored the lovely walled garden with its unique round corner ice houses and created a lake near the harbour shore, stocking it with ducks and geese.

The Friends act as wardens in the park and maintain a refreshment kiosk to help their fund raising. The greenhouses have also been restored and the produce grown in them is sold to help the funding. Work is now in progress to restore the magnificent interior of the house.

Christopher Spurrier built Upton House in 1818 in the Italian style. No expense was spared. A west wing was added in 1825, and at this time the ancient turnpike road between Poole and Wareham was diverted away from the house to enlarge the parkland.

Although less than three miles from the noisy town centre of Poole, the park is one of the most peaceful corners of Dorset except on the days of the twice-yearly Country Fayres, which have become colourful dates on the social calendar.

The Friends are proud of the nature trail which they have prepared. This starts by the old sundial on the terrace at the south side of the house, with views down the sloping lawns over the upper reaches of Poole Harbour and little Pergins Island. Leaving a sweet gum tree and a tall redwood tree, the explorer follows the trail through the heather garden, which also features conifers and rock roses. There is a pets' graveyard near here, with about a dozen gravestones commemorating dogs which belonged to the families who have lived at Upton over the last century.

The trail leads through a walled garden, no longer used for sheltering vegetable beds and exotic fruit trees, but now cleared as a space for fetes and barbecues. In winter it is used as a shelter for livestock. Along the harbour shore, the trail leads between a freshwater marsh and a saltmarsh. Rice grass covering the acres of mudflats prevents access to the boating channels, and provides shelter for saltmarsh birds.

Among the farm animals which can be seen on the walk are Dorset Horn and Suffolk sheep, and Shetland ponies.

Upton House, with its Ionic portico, is notable for its curving colonnaded screens on either side of the main block. Inside, the house has a well-proportioned central hall paved with black marble and Portland stone, rising the full height of the building and lit by a domed lantern. The walls of some of the rooms are decorated with fine art nouveau wallpapers, and the ceilings are in Adam style plaster work.

The Llewellins came to Upton in 1901, when William Llewellin bought it. He later became High Sheriff of the County. One of his sons, Lord Llewellin, became first Governor General of the Rhodesias and Nyasaland, and his daughter Mary was Poole's first ever lady Mayor in 1951. Among other interesting people who lived at Upton were Roger Tichbourne — the Tichbourne Claimant of the infamous Victorian lawsuit — and Carol of Hohenzollern, Prince of Rumania.

The house from the north

The pets' cemetery

# BROWNSEA ISLAND

Open: 31 March - 30 Sept
10.00 - 8.00 (or dusk if
earlier)

Price guide B (does not
include boat trip)

Guided tour daily 2.30
(contact
Dorset Naturalists' Trust
Warden)

Viewed from the dominating heights of the Purbeck Hills, Brownsea looks little more than an enormous mass of river weed floating in Poole harbour, yet this little thickly-wooded island is famous the world over.

The National Trust now cares for Brownsea and protects its wildlife, which includes the rare red squirrel. Nevertheless, visitors who come by boat from Poole Quay and Sandbanks Ferry are free to roam all over its slopes and discover its lonely beaches.

Brownsea was not always so accessible. For many decades the island was privately owned, the last custodian being Mrs Bonham-Christie, a recluse who lived alone in Brownsea Castle, allowed no-one access, and employed a Continental woman of great strength to physically throw trespassers off the island. Today there is no such danger, and only the castle, now a staff club for a large chain store organisation, is barred to the general public.

To fully enjoy your visit, it is worth knowing a few facts about the island's long and varied history.

It once belonged to the monks of Cerne Abbas, was inhabited briefly by the passing Romans, and attacted by Canute. Henry VIII built a square blockhouse on its seaward tip to protect Poole, a fort which eventually became the castle we know today. Queen Elizabeth I granted Brownsea to Sir Christopher Hatton, who was hated by Poole men because he claimed dues on all ships entering the harbour. In 1589 he opened fire on the barque *Bountiful Gift* which was defying his rules, and killed the captain and one of the crew.

A Brownsea peacock

There have been two major fires on Brownsea. The castle was destroyed by fire in 1896, but rebuilt the following year. In the 1930s, when in the hands of the late Mrs Bonham-Christie, a forest fire raged from end to end of the island, and firemen had to force their way ashore with mobile pumps. The blackened island took many years to restore itself.

Colonel William Petrie Waugh bought the island in 1852, wrongly believing that he could mine the richest china clay in England. He spent £10,000 on the church, restored the castle, and went bankrupt.

It is an event which took place in 1907 which has earned Brownsea international fame. On the western shore, General Baden-Powell hoisted a Union Jack on a staff between a handful of tents, and with 20 boys established the Boy Scout movement. The boys came from varied backgrounds ranging from Eton and Harrow to various elementary schools. The first four patrols were organised — Curlews, Wolves, Ravens and Bulls — and on this lonely island they learned to live with each other, to fend for themselves and cultivate comradeship. By the end of a fortnight the General was so encouraged that he set to work to launch scouting worldwide.

The boat trip to Brownsea

Today the island is an excellent place to spend a day, either picnicking or taking meals in the National Trust cafe. Visitors can use the hides to watch for rare water birds, and listen to the calls of peacocks on lawns which, in spring, are carpeted with daffodils. On the western shore the Boy Scouts still come to camp at this Mecca of the Scouting movement.

The church of St Mary is seldom used but is an interesting museum piece. Col. Waugh's reconstruction in the 1850s kept the 13th-century chancel. Under the tower is a family pew with fireplace. The ceiling of the family pew and some screens are said to have come from Crosby Hall in London, and there is a Netherland influence in this building. Amongst the monuments are memorials to two previous owners: the recumbent figure of Charles Van Raalte, dated 1901, and an Italian Quattrocento Madonna, by which to remember William George Cavendish Bentinck who died in 1909.

The quaint line of quayside buildings are typically early 19th century, and do not be fooled by the ancient-looking white stucco octagonal turrets with painted windows at the pierhead. They were built in 1852.

For two weeks in summer Shakespeare's plays are produced at an open-air theatre, but if you come at such a time be sure you bring a mosquito repellent.

# UP THE RIVER TO WAREHAM

The early invaders of our shores came up the river to Wareham when it was the main port in Poole Harbour. This is the way the Danes came, the grinding of their oars echoing across the upper reaches of the harbour until they turned into the river Frome and, cloaked by the tall reeds, sneaked in to pillage and burn the town. This is the way the colourful Roman galleys came to conquer, and today this is the way the pleasure boats from Poole Quay come, bearing happy children and holidaymakers, probably on their first sea adventure. But they arrive in friendship — to take tea, or perhaps a pint of ale at the New Inn by the little harbour wall.

Once in Wareham channel, leaving the new commercial docks and the Royal Marine base hard to starboard, the voyager enters an expanse of water and coast that has changed little over the centuries. He progresses through Middle Mud, Balls Lake and the oyster beds, past Patchins Point and Arne skulking in its own little bay. Somewhere here Poole men once landed to storm Corfe Castle across the sullen heath. They are lonely waters, where the wind whistles through the reeds and gulls and cormorants make plain their annoyance at the intrusion before flying off across the water.

Nearby, Victorian militiamen fired cannon-balls in practice at a target on the tip of Brownsea and later, when gales kept them in harbour, the fishermen dredged them up and sold them to the ironworks at Poole. Today Royal Marine landing craft daily speed up the channel in training. The boatmen who bring visitors up the river to Wareham will tell of the cordite factory, built to supply the army with explosives, which once stood on the shores of Lytchett Bay, and how Sir Malcolm Campbell, testing his last *Bluebird* in 1947, nearly ran aground at 100 mph.

The boatmen will also point out the tiny stone on the shore of Redcliffe Attwell, which marks the boundary of Poole. This was established in 1364, when the Barons of Winchelsea issued a certificate confirming the harbour fishing limits and town boundaries. These were disputed by the men of Wareham, however, and the bitterness between the two towns sharing the same harbour often caused fighting during the years which followed. Wareham regularly accused Poole of moving the boundary to enlarge its fishing area, so since Stuart times the Mayor of Poole, who is also Admiral of the Port, has periodically perambulated the harbour in his barge to watch a jury 'beat the bounds' and reaffirm that the boundaries are in order. Another fleet, headed by the Mayor of Wareham, has always sailed down to meet the Poole procession at Redcliffe Attwell to challenge the Admiral and complain of poaching fishermen.

In recent times the ceremony has taken place every three years, and has become a water carnival in which rival gangs of pirates attempt to board the Admiral's barge and are made to walk the plank at the end of the day.

The large marina which surprises you when turning a bend in the Frome river just before entering Wareham was formerly Ridge Wharf, where Pike's railway brought china clay from the Purbeck pits for loading on to the barges. Steam and diesel powered trains used the wharf until the 1960s.

At the end of the boat trip the voyager steps ashore at Wareham Quay, in one of the oldest ports in the country, a town steeped in history. The round trip takes about four hours and starting times at Pottery steps at Poole Quay are governed by tidal considerations.

Wareham Quay

# WAREHAM

Museum open weekdays
10.00 - 1.00; 2.00 - 5.00

Wareham is a walled town which still contains most of its dwellings within its ancient earthen ramparts. At first sight it is a disappointment but, after some exploration, the traveller becomes strangely drawn to this place.

The town was planned and fortified during the reign of Alfred the Great in the late ninth century, and in spite of its antiquity its narrow roads and lanes are laid out with almost New York-style precision. The four main streets form a perfect cross at the town centre and are appropriately named East, West, North and South Street. There is no earth wall on the south side of the town. The river Frome, which in ancient times was wider and deeper, formed the southern boundary in Saxon days when it was an important port. The silting of the river eventually caused trading vessels to favour Poole but, in the 20th century, Wareham harbour draws many yachtsmen to the quayside. This is a good place to start a walk round the town because the quay is surrounded by car parks.

The Lady St Mary church, built in the 19th century on the site of a Saxon building, is near the river. The Priory is adjacent to it, but reveals nothing of its 12th-century origins. Walking into South Street you come across the Black Bear Inn, a welcome sight to thirsty travellers. Built in 1800, it has windows and a columned porch which carries a black bear. At the crossroads is the Town Hall of 1870, which has been described as 'a wretchedly mean affair', but you notice it because of its dominating clock tower. Across the road is another fine hostelry — The Red Lion, rebuilt in 1762 after a disastrous fire.

A pole lathe in the museum

St Martin's on the Wall is Wareham's showpiece, standing where the north wall is cut away to allow traffic from the east to enter the town over the causeway. Wareham's other river, the Piddle, flows under a bridge here.

Some parts of this lovely church are dated to the year 1020 and there is a Saxon window in one wall. There are traces of 12th-century painting on the north wall of the chancel, and the north aisle was added at that time. The saddle-backed tower is believed to be 16th-century.

Lawrence of Arabia's effigy in St Martin's on the Wall

The building has that peculiar churchy smell of age, and dramatic shafts of light through the open door spotlight the recumbent effigy of Lawrence of Arabia, clad in Arab costume and resting on a camel saddle. Looking very new in this ancient place, it was the work of Eric Kennington in 1935.

For the gruesome-minded, a walk along the walls brings the visitor to the Bloody Bank, the execution place used for participants in the Monmouth Rebellion of 1685, who were tried and condemned by Judge Jeffreys.

Wareham museum makes up in quality what it lacks in quantity. At its new home in East Street, near the Town Hall, the curator, Lorna Pascall, has two unique and valuable collections in her care: a set of silver pennies made at the Wareham Mint in 978, and a pictorial history of Lawrence of Arabia who lived and died at nearby Morton, which is claimed to be the finest collection of its kind in existence. Travellers come from all over the world to see it. The museum also features a display of the archaeology and local history of the town.

# ARNE

The path over the heath near Shipstal Point

Open Whitsun - early Sept.

Although far from the battlefields of Europe, ancient Arne, hidden on heathland in a quiet corner of Poole's lovely harbour, suffered more damage than many French villages in the 1940s because it was a battle training ground, and soldiers stormed ashore on the beaches and fought in the village itself.

It is a credit to the planners that they have not only rebuilt Arne, but it has become designated as an Area of Outstanding Natural Beauty. The dedicated explorer will have to obtain permission from the Royal Society for the Protection of Birds warden, who lives at Wareham, to visit certain parts of the reserve.

However, there is plenty to enjoy and admire for those who just wish to wander in a beautiful place. Arne is reached by turning left along Nutcrack Lane off the A351 at Stoborough, just over the causeway out of Wareham.

In 1952, a claylined vat and other signs of occupation were found in the vicinity, which suggest industrial activities throughout the Roman period. This could have been the place where the domestic pottery was produced which found its way far north to be used by those who built Hadrian's Wall. There is also evidence on the Arne Heath of salt-making using sea water during the Roman period.

It is two miles across this lovely heath to Arne, and beautiful in any season; bright with golden gorse in spring, carpeted with the purple of summer heather, yet perhaps even more beautiful in winter, in russet hues, lonely and asleep.

As you approach the Reserve — twelve hundred acres of woods, heath and moor — notices warn that this part can only be entered with a permit. Ling, cross-leaved heath and bell heather grow here in abundance, together with the lesser-known variety of heather, Dorset heath. Here also is sacred ground for the elusive Dartford warbler and many other birds including nightjars and meadowpipits.

There is a large car park at the entrance to the village. The rebuilt cottages surround the church of St Nicholas, built on a hillock, with nave and chancel in one. A footpath takes the explorer to Shipstal Point, three quarters of a mile away on the shores of Poole Harbour. It was an offloading place for 20th-century smugglers just after the last war. There is a nature trail, part of the Arne Reserve, laid out for visitors to use during the period from May to September, and a leaflet is provided.

The walk takes visitors through a wood and along the edge of a saltmarsh. The beach is quiet except for the calls of seabirds such as the fork-tailed common tern, and the cormorants which perch on the rocks and mooring buoys, spreading their wings to dry. The trail then proceeds to high ground with magnificent views of Corfe, the harbour islands and Poole, with its prominent power station, before looping back to rejoin the path from the car park.

# PURBECK AND LULWORTH

# THE BLUE POOL

Open March - November
Price guide B

All this beauty has evolved from a 50-foot hole that was once a clay pit, filled with rainwater and water which has seeped in from the surrounding clay. The placid pool still has clay in it, and there is a high concentration of minerals and clay suspended in the water. No waterweed or microscopic vegetation lives in the pool, so there is very little oxygen - consequently there are no fish. The combination of these factors imparts to the water the unique properties of transmission, diffraction and reflection of light which so delight those who sit on the pool's banks.

To see the pool at its best, walk clockwise along the 'high road', a path which allows you to look down on the pool, and passes through beautiful woodland. Flights of steps lead down to the edge of the water and little beaches at various points.

Fifty years ago, the vegetation was sparse - a light covering of gorse and heather and few trees. The woodlands have 'just growed' since then. Now you may meet squirrels, badgers and deer, including some Japanese Sika deer which swam across the sea from Brownsea Island in Poole Harbour.

The formation of one of Purbeck's unique and most colourful attractions, the Blue Pool, is closely associated with one of the Isle's main industries — the mining of the famous ball clay, favoured by the great pottery manufacturer Josiah Wedgwood, and used by the potteries of Worcester, Derby, Minton and Spode.

Visitors come to the Blue Pool, situated at Furzebrook off the Stoborough to Corfe Castle road, because of its beauty and peacefulness. A sheet of water, sometimes rich turquoise, sometimes sapphire blue, it is surrounded by 25 acres of heather, gorse, pine trees and silver birches on sloping banks.

A complete circuit of the pool gives views of the water from every angle, in a variety of shades and moods framed through the trees. The place is a challenge to artist and photographer alike, never seems crowded and has an atmosphere of such peace that visitors return time and time again.

Sit on one of the benches placed at strategic points and you may see a rare Dartford warbler amongst the birdlife, or a sand lizard, one of the rarest British reptiles. Or just sit and rest in this lovely place and contemplate the pool's ever-changing chameleon-like character. You need not retrace your steps because, if you carry on, you eventually arrive back at the entrance and the tea lawns, where the speciality is home-made sponge cake.

Three families have owned the land around Furzebrook in 400 years. In 1578, John Brown and John Batten purchased 1000 acres from Christopher Percy. Brown kept the eastern third for himself and this became Furzebrook Estate. It is not known how early clay was mined here but, in 1660, a grandson, Thomas Brown, was selling clay for tobacco pipes.

The Blue Pool was dug in 1840 and the property sold to the Pike Brothers in 1874. They pulled down the farmhouse and built Furzebrook House. The last of the family to live there died in 1929, and in 1934 the site was bought by Mr Barnard. The Blue Pool, with its tea rooms, gift shop, garden centre and aviary, is now under the supervision of Miss Jennifer Barnard, his elder daughter.

# CORFE CASTLE

Castle open March to Oct inclusive, daily 10.00-6.00; Nov to Feb inclusive, Sat-Sun 2.00-4.00

Price guide B

Museum open daily 9.00-6.00

Corfe Castle, a crumbled citadel, centrepiece of a village which looks like a film set, must be Dorset's most famous attraction — and film set it was for the television adaptation of Thomas Hardy's *The Mayor of Casterbridge*. Telephone wires and television aerials were removed and extra houses built in plastics. A replica of Dorchester's town pump was created in glass fibre, to provide the finishing touch to the transformation of Corfe into the county town of Casterbridge (Dorchester). The proud populace, as if aware of their responsibility to care for a unique and beautiful place, smartened up the grey stone cottages, weighed down by heavy sagging stone roofs, and coaxed jasmine and colourful creepers around the doors, filled the gardens with old-world flowers such as fuchsias, hollyhocks and snapdragons, and planted the verges with banks of daffodils.

Corfe's three main streets converge on a square where the church and two splendid inns face each other. If you arrive by car, turn into the Square where there is parking space. If this is full, a large car park is provided a few hundred yards along West Street. Near the Square is a model of the Castle in its complete state and it is probably best to visit this first to learn something of the geography of the Castle.

Across the road at this point is the Town Hall, a little oddity. The downstairs room of this building, dated 1774, is now a museum. Around the corner, on the south side of the Square, is the Town House (now the National Westminster Bank) with three bays. The centre one is bowed out strangely with a round-headed window in the upper part of the bow. This was the Mayor's robing room, which could be entered from the high level churchyard — a reminder that Corfe in the 16th century was a town of consequence, and returned two members of Parliament until 1832. The smallness of the Town Hall shows how Corfe's importance had dwindled by the 18th century. The Greyhound Hotel, beneath the castle ruin, was built in 1733 and has a porch over the pavement supported by Tuscan columns.

The memorial to Edward the Martyr

The 1860 church of St Edward is large for so small a place and retains some of the earlier 13th-century work. The view of the Castle from West Street near the church is breathtaking. It stands aloft above the irregular roof levels of the lovely Purbeck cottages with their dormer windows standing out like half-closed eyelids.

The Castle occupies an extraordinary natural position, a steep-sided hillock at the base of a cleft in the spine-like ridge of the Purbeck Hills. The remains of the Norman tower-keep, shattered by mines after its long resistance to Parliament during the Civil Wars, stand on the summit, but the curtain walls and towers lie on the slopes in disarray. No ruin in the country is more imposing, and it can be seen from miles around. Why it was built is still open to speculation, because in spite of its dominating position, it had nothing to defend. It has even been suggested that a castle builder thought it would be a nice place to live.

Retrace your steps to the Church Knowle road just below the village, and climb to the top of the Purbeck Ridge which looks down on castle and village. Sit a while and consider the awful history of this place.

In Saxon times, before the castle was built, there was a hunting lodge on the site and it was here that the widowed Queen Elfrida lived. Her stepson Edward was king, but she wanted her own son Ethelred to reign. The young King Edward, hunting in Purbeck, called at the lodge for a drink. The Queen brought him a cup of wine and, as he sat astride his horse drinking it, a servant plunged a dagger into his back. He galloped off across the heath toward Wareham but soon fell dying from the saddle, to be dragged, foot stirrup, to the site of a house now called St Edward's Cottage. He was buried at Wareham and later reburied with ceremony at Shaftesbury. The murdered king was canonised as Edward The Martyr, and Queen Elfrida retired in remorse to a nunnery at Bere Regis.

There was further evil in the days of King John, who sent 24 knights who had fought for his rival brother Arthur to his castle at Corfe, and starved 22 of them to death. John also imprisoned Prince Arthur's sister Eleanor at Corfe, and Isabel and Margery, daughters of the King of Scotland. Another of John's misdeeds concerned Peter of Pomfret, who was taken from a dungeon at Corfe and dragged behind a horse to Wareham where he was hanged.

In the 17th century, the castle came into the hands of Sir John Bankes, and it was during his time that Corfe became a ruin. When the Civil War came in the 1640s, Sir John Bankes prepared his castle for service to the King, and it was twice besieged. It so happened that, during one attack, Sir John was away and Lady Bankes, her maids and servants beat back the 150 Poole seamen who tried to scale the steep banks, by pouring hot ashes and boiling oil over them. Eventually the castle fell because of the treachery of an officer of the garrison who opened the gate at nightfall. Parliament ordered it to be blown up, but the strong walls were defiant and, after well over three centuries, there is still enough castle left to form a monument to the builders of the day.

If your exploration of Corfe occurs on Shrove Tuesday, you will witness a strange custom in the ancient streets. To preserve their rights of way, Purbeck quarrymen kick a football through the village. New apprentices to the Purbeck Stone Cutters and Marblers have to carry a quart of ale and small loaf from the Fox Inn to the Town Hall. It sounds easy, but thirsty veterans stand in the road and constantly steal the ale. The Fox is an interesting inn with quaint little bars and a serving-hatch pierced through an 18-inch wall. It was standing 100 years before the castle was blown up in 1645.

# THE
# INTERNATIONALLY FAMOUS
## HOTEL & RESTAURANT

# CHEWTON GLEN HOTEL

New Milton
Hampshire
England  BH25 6QS
Telephone: Highcliffe (04252) 5341  Telex: 41456

# BALL CLAY MINING

Producers of china clay do not welcome visitors. Like those who manufacture the paper on which five-pound notes are printed, their activities are shrouded in secrecy. So the explorer can only see the exterior of the Purbeck ball clay mines, and the occasional section of rusty track — relics of the days when clay by the ton was brought by trains and trams to Poole Harbour shores.

The mining of ball clay has been a major Dorset industry for two centuries, but its history goes back far longer than that. In the first century AD, the Romans at Wareham discovered the clay and made domestic pots and tiles for their villas. In the Middle Ages monks from local abbeys worked the clay and made utensils for their kitchens and tiles for the abbey roofs.

Strangely, it was a plant brought to this country in the 16th century which most affected the lives and fortunes of the Purbeck clay miners. Sir Walter Raleigh introduced tobacco, and from then on there was an enormous demand for clay to make tobacco pipes. By 1690, 10,000 tons had been exported from Poole for their manufacture.

In the middle of the 18th century a great expansion of the industry took place, due to the demand for fine china and porcelain to decorate the great country houses which were being built, coupled with the popularity of tea and coffee and the need for elegant tea and coffee services.

Ridge Wharf today

In 1750 a Mr Rhodes from Poole began to sell 10-inch cubes of clay known as 'clay balls' to Staffordshire potters, but it was mainly the example of Josiah Wedgewood that encouraged the Midlands potters to use the fine clays from the Purbeck Peninsular. With pride, Purbeck men recall that Wedgewood's 1,000 piece Russian service, made for the Empress Catherine of Russia, was made from clay mined very near the Blue Pool.

Three families were responsible for the development of the Purbeck industry. Thomas Hyde was successful in the 1770s owing to a contract with Wedgewood, but his business failed in 1792.

Benjamin Fayle, a London potter, revolutionised the distribution system of the day. Dissatisfied with the inefficient use of donkeys and horses and carts, he introduced a mineral line in 1806 known as Fayle's Tramway. This linked the Norden clay pits near Corfe Castle to a jetty at Middlebere in Poole Harbour. He started with horse-drawn wooden wagons and mechanised the line in 1878. This tramway closed in 1905, but a new line opened the same year which linked Norden with Fayles clay works at Newton. This already had a railway and ships at Goathorn Pier near Poole Harbour entrance. It was not until 1937 that the Newton Clay works declined and the line was abandoned. A bridle path now follows this route.

The Pike Brothers from Devon, prospecting for clay, came and purchased Furzebrook House in 1760, and dug a pit almost at their back door which is now known as the Blue Pool. In 1866 they introduced their own mechanised transport system. The Pike Railway linked Furzebrook to Ridge Wharf on the Frome just below Wareham, now a busy yachting marina. Wooden wagons were used throughout the system which lasted through the age of steam and diesel until the 1960s.

In 1949, Fayles and Pikes merged, but the company has since been absorbed into English China Clays whose subsidiary EEC Ball Clay Ltd operate from Wareham.

Why ball clay? you may ask. The clay used to be dug with tubals, a type of spade, giving rise to the name ball clay. Excavators and pneumatic spades are used today and although wooden wagons still bring the clay to the surface, lorries now transport it to the works at Furzebrook.

Visits to the workings are not permitted except in specialist parties, the old workings have been flattened, and present sites have been screened and landscaped. The last of the rail tracks have recently been removed; even so the interested explorer can wander through the old cuttings to such places as Ridge Wharf, Middlebere, and Goathorn, even though the routes may be barred in some places by the sites of a new type of prospecting — oil exploration.

# STUDLAND

Whichever way you approach Studland, the route is beautiful. The descents from the hills behind Swanage, or from the Purbeck range which runs up to Corfe Castle, offer breathtaking views on a summer's day. Poole Harbour, Bournemouth and a great expanse of Channel, with the Isle of Wight marking the Solent entry, lie before you. From the east the visitors pour off the Sandbanks ferry and fan out across virgin heath and dunes. But Studland has remained unimpressed by its importance as a pleasure spot for nearby town dwellers, and there is no noticeable centre and no planning. Motoring through, the stranger could miss this enchanting place with its little lanes, lovely walks and sandy beach. If you arrive by boat to picnic on the beach, there is no sign of the village which hides among the trees.

Looking west from Old Harry Rocks

The Norman church of St Nicholas

The explorer must wander in every lane or he will miss the old Manor Farm and Manor House with their colourful medley of stone roofs, the remains of the Saxon Cross, and the church of St Nicholas — one of the most complete of Norman village churches. All Norman, in fact, except the Early English windows and other windows enlarged in the 18th century, and the south porch. Its rare beauty is the central tower, standing as the Normans left it — unfinished because of a problem with settlement of the foundations. Above the vaulted ceiling of the sanctuary is a priest's room, approached by a door high up on the outside wall.

The churchyard has a beautiful view of the cliffs near Old Harry Rocks. Among the lichen-covered gravestones is that of Sgt William Lawrence of the 40th Regiment of Foot. On the stone's other side is the name of Clotilde Clairet of Germain-en-Lay, the Frenchwoman he lost his heart to and brought home to Studland, after warring with the French for a decade.

Sgt Lawrence fought in most of Wellington's battles and, in 1805, was in South America fighting Spaniards who were allies of the French. He volunteered for the storming of Badajos and was severely wounded. He completed his war experiences at the Battle of Waterloo in 1815 and marched to Paris. There he fell in love with Clotilde and married her. They kept a small inn at Studland for 38 years, until she died. He survived her by 16 years and his wish for a military funeral was carried out 54 years after Waterloo.

The Manor House, now an hotel, was built in 1825 as a marine villa, but the many additions and alterations made by its former owner, the Rt. Hon. George Bankes, give the building a strange, picturesque appearance. Architecturally it is totally disorganised. It stands on a corner near the Bankes Arms, where you can lunch before attempting the mile-long walk along the clifftop to the Old Harry Rocks.

Over 200 acres of this land — Ballard Down — belongs to the National Trust and is noted as a Site of Special Scientific Interest by the Nature Conservancy Council. Ballard Down is at the eastern end of the chalk range which extends from Lulworth, and once continued to the Isle of Wight, across the bay. The famous Old Harry Rocks on the point were once part of this range. The chalk and greensand exposed in the cliffs contain fossils of extinct sea creatures which can be collected from fallen rocks on the beaches.

Although the woodlands have been depleted by Dutch elm disease, the call of the woodpecker is still heard and, among a variety of seabirds, flocks of Canada geese glean for food in the fields before returning to Poole Park and Brownsea. They have now taken over Poole Park. The author remembers when two pairs were introduced there about 20 years ago.

Among the dunes between Studland and the Poole Harbour entrance is a N.N.R. Heath Reserve, and explorers are asked to keep to the trail paths.

On the heath, about a mile from the village, are the Agglestone and Puckstone. The former is about 18 feet high and about 80 round and weighs 400 tons. Although surrounded by many legends, including the story that the Devil threw them from the Isle of Wight when trying to hit Old Harry, the simple fact is that they are hardened formations which have not eroded as the rest of the heath has worn down.

# DURLSTON PARK

Anvil Point lighthouse

Centre open daily Easter -
end Oct 10.30 - 5.30

Long before the days of nature trails and country parks, Durlston Head above Swanage was a popular rendezvous for walkers. Here on the clifftops, the seabirds scream overhead and wheel down to land on the ledges below, and the invigorating sea breezes sweep in to revitalise the visitor.

Durlston Park, which covers 261 acres, was opened by the Dorset County Council in 1973. It is an area of beautiful coast encompassing the Anvil Point Lighthouse and the clifftop castle. Much of the Park is within the Dorset Area of Outstanding Natural Beauty and recognised as part of our Heritage Coastline. The wartime radar station and camp has been adapted to make a large car park and there is an information centre where illustrated leaflets are available on individual topics. Stone, insects, trees, birds and flowers are among the subjects covered. To protect the animals, trees and birds, the cliffs from Tilly Whim Caves to Durlston Head are maintained as a wildlife sanctuary. Picnic tables are grouped near the car parks and along the path to the lighthouse and, because parking is concentrated in one area, visitors can explore the rich countryside without all the incursions of modern urban life.

The warden will show you the area on a model at the information centre and hand out a leaflet which plans three separate walks. One, a short easy route, is for those who cannot walk long distances. Sadly the interesting walk underground in the Tilly Whim Caves is no longer possible, beacause the cost of making them safe is prohibitive. However, you can see the cave entrances which open out to the stone ledges, from which cranes lowered the quarried stone into barges at the bottom of the cliff over 150 years ago.

The Great Globe

For those who wish to stay near the coast and follow part of the great coastal footpath, there is much to see. Descending from the car park, the visitor encounters Durlston Castle — built by George Burt during the 1880s — which contains some of the curious stone panels bearing inscriptions which are frequently seen in the Swanage area. The stones here are engraved with information such as the distances of major cities of the world from Swanage. Further down the slope is the Great Globe, 40 tons of Portland limestone carved in the shape of the Earth. Ten feet in diameter, it was placed there in 1887.

The cliff path leads to the lighthouse at Anvil Point, built by Trinity House in 1881. Recently made automatic, it is visible for 18 miles. Eventually the path leads into wilder terrain, and is more difficult to walk, but it offers fine views of St Aldhelm's Head.

The area swarms with insect and butterfly life, and in May you will see the small copper, whose wings look like burnished copper, and the tiny dingy and grizzled skippers. The rare, local Lulworth skippers appear later in the summer. Bird lovers will look for the wheatear, meadow pipit, stonechat and willow warbler, and there is a great variety of seabirds living on the cliff face, including kittiwakes, fulmars and guillemots.

Tilly Whim Caves

# SWANAGE

The little bay of Swanage, with its doorstep-sized promenade, overlooked by towering white cliffs, is the epitome of the English Victorian seaside resort. The pleasing shopping centre is composed of two streets which link near the sea to form a tidy town, easy to explore and all within easy reach of the beach and bay.

It was a young man with a Dick Whittington life story who gave an architectural face to Swanage. Poor boy John Mowlem, who had worked in the Tilly Whim quarries just down the coast, begged a sea captain engaged in transporting stone and marble to give him passage to London. He had only nine pence in his pocket.

In London he made good, eventually became a leading contractor (does the name Mowlem ring a bell?) and made a vast fortune. He paved the streets of London, not with gold, but Purbeck marble. But John never forgot his home town and, as he helped rebuild a modern London with Dorset stone, he sent home strange ballast cargoes in return. This is why, until recently, grand lamp standards lined the Swanage seafront bearing such crests as Soho and St Martin's in the Fields. Cannon barrels from Sebastapol, captured during the Crimean War, served as bollards at street ends.

The old lamp standards gave way to uninteresting modern concrete posts a few years ago, but much of the stonework removed from famous London buildings and re-erected in Swanage has become part of the town's heritage.

The strange faceless clock tower, which stands on the shore among the boats and fishing nets near the lifeboat house, once graced the southern approach to London Bridge. It had been erected as a memorial to the Duke of Wellington, but it obstructed the traffic which was becoming a problem even in the late 19th century. It had to be removed, so Mowlem dismantled it and brought it to Swanage. The actual clock — which had always been a bad timekeeper — never arrived, so the faces were filled with windows.

The Mowlem touch is evident in the bustling High Street which climbs up from the seafront. The elegant frontage of the Town Hall was designed by Edward Jarman in 1680 — not for the Town Hall, but for the Mercers' Hall in Cheapside, London. It is a most ornate facade. Fine mouldings and rich scrolls adorn it and, over the door, resting on two cherub heads and with angels floating on either side, there is a flower-crowned bust of the Madonna.

Higher up the hill is Purbeck House, dominating the street, now the Convent of Mercy. Built in 1875, the style is High Victorian and not architecturally pleasant. It is largely hidden behind high walls built right to the pavement. The house was built for George Burt, a nephew of John Mowlem, and another of the town's benefactors.

The parish church of St Mary with (left) the old refectory

In the grounds are more pieces salvaged from Mowlem's London escapades. The most important pieces are an archway originally erected at Hyde Park Corner in 1844 as the entrance to Green Park, and, in a specially-contrived patio to the south-east of the house, six cast-iron columns from Bunning's short-lived Billingsgate Market, and three 17th-century statues from the Royal Exchange.

Probably Mowlem's best-known gift is the stone globe, set up by George Burt at Durlston Castle. Forty tons of Portland stone, it stands on the cliffside overlooking the Channel.

The town's benefactor was also responsible for creating the picturesque millpond surrounded by cottages on a hillside near the parish church.

Behind the Town Hall is the old town lock-up, not much larger than an outside privy. The stone building bears a strange inscription stating that it was erected by friends of religion for the prevention of vice and immorality.

Swanage was a well-known smuggling centre, the quarried cliffs with access to the sea making ideal hiding places. There are still one or two old Purbeck stone cottages on the seafront which may have sheltered smugglers from the revenue men.

The Town Hall - designed in 1680, re-erected in Swanage in 1883

Although St Mary's parish church is a large, mainly 19th and 20th-century building, the solid-looking tower is said to be older than Corfe Castle. It is 74 feet high, and long before it had its bells, it did duty as a military watch tower. The oldest of the eight bells is dated 1594.

On the seafront, near the modern Mowlem Theatre and restaurant, is a column commemorating the day in the year 877 when the Danish fleet, fleeing from Alfred, was shattered on the sharp rocks of Peveril Ledge which runs seaward underwater from the tip of Peveril Point. Many other ships have been lost here including a Spanish ship belonging to the Armada. But today a bobbing buoy at the seaward end of this obstruction is a navigational aid to sailors. Three cannon balls form the top of the commemorative column — rather inappropriate because the disaster took place many years before gunpowder was invented.

Near the millpond and next to the church is the Tithe Barn Museum. An excellent display includes maps of the area with the underground quarries, relevant photographs and examples of the tiles and uses of stones quarried, and a few fine polished carvings in stone taken from some of the harder layers. There are also exhibits of quarrying tools (on loan by kind permission of the Quarry Preservation Society) and a display of model ships, authentic and true to scale, as used in exporting stone from Swanage.

The millpond

It is hoped to eventually re-open the Bell Vue Stone Quarry, near Priests Way, South of Herston, as a working industrial museum. The original quarry houses are still on the site.

Many explorers will enjoy sitting on the green slopes of Peveril Point on the south side of the beautiful bay. They may care to ponder on Swanage's picturesque past, when the bay was full of ships awaiting the stone and marble which was brought down from the hills and loaded from horse-drawn carts — the horses often wading into the water. Then, in the early 1800s, came the holiday boom. Queen Victoria came and popularised it as a resort and a new invasion of ships began, as paddle steamers brought visitors from resorts all along the coast, swelling the numbers of those who arrived by the new railway.

Now that has all changed. Swanage has lost its commercial railway, the paddle steamers are no longer a viable proposition and, at the time of writing, neither of the two piers are considered safe for the public.

Yet Swanage is still beautiful, peaceful and a joy to visit, and the Dorset Naturalists' Trust has recently opened the Townsend Nature Reserve — 32 acres of unspoilt hillside a few minutes walk from the High Street, which commands a view of the town and the chalk ridge of the Purbeck Hills which overlooks it.

# SWANAGE RAILWAY

Running hours: 11.30-4.30
Price guide C

The little branch-line trains which chugged to outposts of Dorset were mostly lost during Beeching's decimation of our railway system, but the people of Swanage, loath to lose their link with the main line at Wareham, fought desperately to retain their railway in spite of the fact that BR removed much of the track. Today, enthusiasts have not only relaid some of the line, but the steam train has returned to become one of the attractions of this charming Victorian resort.

The original line, opened in 1885 from Wareham via Corfe Castle to Swanage, was a latecomer on the English railway scene, but it rapidly prospered and served the people well in peace and war until it was closed in January 1972 — in spite of the opposition of thousands of people, both local and national.

Since that sad day, the struggle to reopen the branch has been pushed forward by the Swanage Railway Project. In spite of formidable problems, two miles of track have been relaid to passenger standards, Swanage Station has been restored to a better state than in BR days, steam locomotives and diesel shunters have been acquired, carriage stock including a Brighton Belle Pullman (No. 88) gleams and a restaurant car is in operation. The goods shed, engine shed, turntable and coaling dock have all been restored, and the railway has become a mecca for enthusiast and layman alike.

The Swanage Railway Project consists of several organisations. The Swanage Railway Co. Ltd. builds and operates the railway. The Swanage-Wareham Railway Group, locally based but with national and international membership, looks after fund-raising, publicity and local support. Locomotives, carriages and wagons are put at the disposal of the project by the Southern Steam Trust (a registered charity), which is particularly interested in SR artefacts, and the LMS/GWR Group provides rolling stock which was originally built for those railways. The common aim is to rebuild the branch to link with BR at Wareham via Corfe Castle, and run an all-the-year-round amenity service with steam tourist trains to Corfe Castle and possibly Blue Pool. There are plans for a Park and Ride scheme to help motorists avoid the daunting traffic problems in the holiday season.

A halt has been built at Herston and the trip from Swanage to Herston and back takes three-quarters of an hour. Trains run every Sunday from June to September, all Bank Holiday weekends and every day during school holidays.

# PURBECK QUARRIES

Open-cast workings at the quarry hamlet of Acton

Coach House
Museum open
April-Sept (inclusive)
Tue, Thur, Sat 2.00-5.00

Parish Museum open
April - Sept (inclusive)
Mon - Sat 9.30 - 12.30;
Sat 9.00 - 1.00 all year

The merits of Purbeck limestone were first exploited by the Romans, who began by quarrying it from natural outcrops. It proved ideal for building handsome villas, temples and public baths, the foundations of which still survive in and around Dorset. Their finest discovery was Purbeck marble — greenish or reddish limestone of the upper oolite in which shells of freshwater snails can be identified. The pattern created by these tiny snail shells when the stone is polished is a large part of its visual attraction.

With the departure of the Romans, and the eventual conversion of their successors to Chritianity, church-building became the main preoccupation of architects. By the year 1100, masons were at work on more than a dozen cathedrals, and Dorset stone in the form of Purbeck marble was to be used in the great majority of these Norman masterpieces. During the 12th, 13th and 14th centuries, Purbeck marble was taken from surface quarries at Wilkswood, Downshay, Afflington and Blashenwell. It was exported in vast quantities, mostly in the form of pillars, in small ships which went by coast and river from Ower Quay on Poole Harbour to Exeter, Salisbury, Winchester, Canterbury, Chichester, Westminster, Lincoln, York and Durham. Corfe became famous all over England as the head-quarters of the Purbeck marble industry.

At some time during the medieval era the quarrymen became organised into the Ancient Order of Purbeck Marblers and Stone Cutters. The actual date of the Order's formation is unknown, because the earliest records were burnt at Corfe Castle in the 16th century. However, copies of a 1551 charter have survived, and they state that the working of the quarries was exclusive to Freemen of the Isle of Purbeck. To be able to take up this privilege, one had to be the legitimate son (or grandson if the line was through a female) of a Freeman, and 21 years of age.

The Order still survives. Each year, on Shrove Tuesday, it meets at Corfe town hall, and after transacting the traditional business, such as the issue of apprenticeship certificates, arbitrations between quarriers, and the election of officers,

the marblers set out with a customary football and a pound of pepper along the old road to Ower Quay, according to a custom intended to preserve the Order's right of way along the thoroughfare.

The difficulty of moving stone from Worth and Corfe to Ower Quay was eventually overcome by establishing quarries nearer the sea at Swanage. Quays were established opposite the present Victoria Hotel — some tracks are still visible — and hundreds of tons of stone went from Swanage to London to pave the streets.

Today regular shipments of stone can still be seen leaving Purbeck, not by sea or rail, but by road. It is used for general house building, bridges and road aggregate. The stone is quarried by modern machinery, a far cry from the old methods when a man had to sink a shaft into the bedrock some 80 to 100 feet underground and dig into the marketable beds of stone, hauling it to the surface to dress and prepare it all by hand.

The J. Suttle Swanage Quarries, reached via the High Street and Priests Road, will show explorers how stone is quarried, but only by pre-arrangement and preferably in parties. Dinosaur tracks were discovered in this quarry in 1963.

There is also a small community clustered round open quarries at Acton, a tiny hamlet seen on the left as you climb the hill to Worth Matravers on the B3069 out of Swanage. The quarrymen are very friendly and will show explorers round these open-cast workings. Two more quarries can be inspected nearby on the right of the B3069.

At Langton Matravers, on the B3069 road out of Swanage which climbs into the quarry hills, is the Coach House Museum in St George's Close beside the parish church, devoted to the Purbeck marble and stone industries over the last 1000 years. It includes exhibits showing the working and living conditions of the quarries of the past. The Parish Museum in the High Street opposite the King's Arms shows the history of Langton Matravers including cottage industries, architecture, farming and personalities.

Dinosaur footprints discovered at the J. Suttle Swanage Quarries in 1963

47

# THE HERITAGE COAST PATH

The coastline of Dorset is one of 30 areas in England and Wales considered by the Countryside Commission to be worthy of protection as Areas of Outstanding Natural Beauty. Most of the work involved in caring for the area is undertaken by the Dorset Naturalists' Trust, and the Trust has prepared a coastal footpath which runs all the way from Poole to Weymouth.

Known as the Heritage Coast Path, the walk has been open since 1974, and provides access to some superb coastal scenery. Long-distance hikers may care to attempt the whole route, but for the less energetic the path from Anvil Point to St Aldhelm's Point provides a fine introduction to one of the most beautiful stretches of coast in southern England.

The path starts at Sandbanks ferry and continues along the shore of Studland Bay and through Swanage, but soon the noise and bustle of the town is left behind and the explorer enters a new world of tranquility. From here the coastal path footpath heads west, and ahead of the walker lie six miles of lonely rockbound coast. Fresh breezes blow off the Channel to set cheeks aglow, and the waves that sweep in from the sea break against precipitous stone cliffs and treacherous-looking ledges. The green heights of Purbeck curve down to the sea where the rugged cliff-face is dotted with quarry entrances resembling giant rabbit-holes.

On a sunny out-of-season morning you can walk for hours along this well-defined path without meeting a living soul. You are alone with the sound of the sea teasing the rocks and the screams of seagulls overhead. Follow the path up and over the undulating clifftop where each well-kept stile has its own milestone. It is a place of sweet-sounding names, like Dancing Ledge, a unique exposed ledge of stone at sea level which provides a bathing place for experienced swimmers. A small natural pool has been cut out of the ledge but it is a dangerous spot on a rising tide.

The rock platform was originally cleared to make a dock for loading stone on to coasters. At the time a wag was supposed to have remarked that the acre of flat rock was big enough for a dance floor; hence the name Dancing Ledge. Others say that it is so named because the waves dance through the rock cracks.

Dancing Ledge can also be reached easily from Langton Matravers. A turning in the village leads to a farm track which can be followed to Spyway Farm, where a friendly farmer allows parking for a small fee. From there it is half a mile across fields to the hill above the ledge.

Because of its loneliness the coast was popular with smugglers, who had a base at Spyway Farm. Once in the 1790s a cargo of brandy was secretly conveyed to the church in Langton and the barrels were concealed between the ceiling and the roof. Unfortunately the ceiling gave way during a service, showering the barrels on the congregation with fatal results.

Continuing along the coastal path Seacombe Cliff lies ahead; at Seacombe Bottom the quarries are vast and once provided ample storage space for contraband. There are also a number of quarries at Winspit, the last point of access to the sea before the heights of St Aldhelm's Head. In winter Winspit can be a bleak place, and it has seen its share of tragedy. It was here that the East Indiaman *Halsewell* foundered in 1786, with the loss of 166 lives.

Dancing Ledge (foreground) and the path to Winspit

The mile-long track to Winspit from Worth Matravers makes a pleasant walk, with excellent views of the medieval strip lynchet cultivation system on the hillside, thought to be the finest example in the country.

Worth Matravers itself, with its neat duckpond, is well worth a deviation from the coastal path. Worth was once bigger than Swanage, and was the home of the Rector of the parish. He would walk down to Swanage along the footpath which is still known as Priest's Way.

The medieval field systems above Winspit

The Heritage Coast Path continues from Winspit to St Aldhelm's Head, and westwards to Weymouth. A further stretch is being prepared from Weymouth to Lyme Regis, but at the time of writing this has not been defined as part of the Heritage Coast Scheme.

# ST ALDHELM'S HEAD AND KIMMERIDGE

Kimmeridge Bay

St Aldhelm's is the dominant headland at the eastern end of Weymouth Bay and the Purbecks. It is 350 feet high and as rugged and forbidding as any part of the Dorset coast. The road from Worth Matravers is a rough track used mainly by the coastguards who have an important look-out on the clifftop. The walk of a mile or so from the car park at Worth Matravers rewards you with magnificent views of the Channel and Portland, wallowing like a great stranded whale across the bay.

At St Aldhelm's, look down at the turbulent race where several tides meet in constant quarrelsome fury. It looked the same when wallowing galleasses and faster caravels came up the Channel in the 16th century, guided by a fiery beacon on the Head, the flames warning of the cruel rocks beneath. The Armada sailed past in 1588 pursued by Drake; and certainly Nelson's fleet, heading for Alderney where ships were stationed to cover Cherbourg. More recently, the coastguards on watch on D-day in June 1944 looked out in the grey light of dawn to see the great Allied invasion fleet pouring out of Poole and Portland, heading towards the beaches of Normandy.

The strange little Norman chapel, 32 feet square, has stood on the cliff for over 700 years. The chapel has walls six feet thick and the interior is dim from the light of a single slit window. Centuries before the modern lighthouses were built along the coast, a priest lived in the chapel, kept a look-out for ships and tended the beacon. It is thought that the beacon once burned in an iron basket or cresset on its roof, but the cresset has now been replaced by a cross.

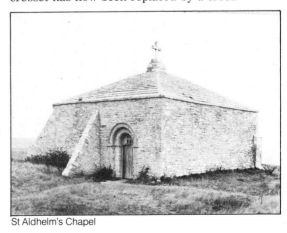

St Aldhelm's Chapel

The coastal path leading down to Kimmeridge Bay

The cliffs below have witnessed many shipwrecks, none more famous than the East Indiaman *Halsewell* in 1786 — a 758-tonner bound for Bombay. A winter westerly washed her ashore at Winspit, just east of St Aldhelm's, crushing her on the rocks beneath the cliff. Some of the passengers and crew struggled ashore on to the ledges and climbed up the cliff, but *Halsewell* quickly broke up leaving many clinging to the cliff face. There were only 74 survivors out of a complement of 240, and some of the dead are buried on the clifftop at Winspit. The terrible tragedy was the inspiration for *The Long Journey*, a story by Charles Dickens. No exploration of Dorset could be complete without half a day spent at St Aldhelm's, often wrongly referred to as St Alban's because the old seamen found it easier to say.

Under the shelter of the great promontory of St Aldhelm's, on the western side, is Chapman's Pool. It can be reached along the cliffs from the Head using the coast footpath, but it is easier to come to this remote Purbeck bay from Kingston, where there is a car park, and walk along a rough track leading down to the Pool. It is pleasanter on the grassy slopes than on the beach, for it is not particularly attractive for bathing with much seaweed in evidence. The bay is used as a haven by fishermen.

The coastal path continues for three miles to Kimmeridge, but most visitors arrive by road from Corfe Castle via Church Knowle and turn off just before the little hamlet of Steeple.

Kimmeridge lies beneath steep hills. The beach is private and, leaving the village of thatched stone houses behind, the explorer is confronted by a toll gate reminiscent of a frontier barrier. However, the people are very friendly and, for a small charge, they will let your car through to the beach for the day, no matter how many passengers.

You either love Kimmeridge for its almost foreign atmosphere, or hate it for its black shale and ledges, which favour the skin diver rather than the bather. It is explorers' country — a place with a long and strange history of commerce.

When the Romans came, they made jet-like jewellery from the bituminous shale in the cliffs. For generations, the little round discs found on the beaches were called coal money, but they were actually cores from the Roman turners' lathes. Some can be seen in Dorchester Museum. In a later attempt to commercialise the shale, Frenchmen shipped it out from the small harbour which once existed, to make lamp oil on the Continent. The venture failed; the Parisians would not use the oil because of the intolerable smell.

Although cut off at the foot of towering hills and with a bay not easy to enter — being wide open to the full force of the south-westerly gales — this little place was the centre of many commercial ventures because the oil-bearing shale could be used to fire furnaces. In the days of Elizabeth I, Sir William Clavell built a harbour and attempted to exploit alum. Unfortunately the enterprise was a disaster, as was the glass works which flourished for a while in the 1700s and ended in ruin. A gale destroyed Clavell's harbour in 1745 and, with it, a defensive position equipped with two cannon. The remains of a later harbour can still be seen, however.

The Clavell Tower

Kimmeridge does not easily accept defeat and, in the 1960s, the first commercial oil well in this country was opened on the cliffs. A nodding donkey has been pumping oil from the Kimmeridge shale ever since.

The Clavell Tower overlooking the bay is a three-storey folly built by the Rev. John Richards Clavell in 1820. Around the bottom is a colonnade of Tuscan columns and, at the top, a parapet pierced with quatrefoils. Nearby are signs of salt-making activities.

The ledges off Kimmeridge have claimed countless fine vessels, particularly in the days of sail, and an important lifeboat station was based there from 1868 to 1896. During that time the Kimmeridge boats saved 18 lives. These were the tough days when the men rowed their boats to stricken vessels. The three boats which served Kimmeridge, all about 30 feet long, together cost £783, whereas a modern lifeboat costs hundreds of thousands.

From St Aldhelm's Head to Kimmeridge is a delightful coastal walk for those who enjoy rough tracks and bracing air. In its entirety the walk takes in about six miles of the Dorset coastal path and is one of the loveliest sections of the Heritage Coast.

# THE RANGE WALKS

The view across Worbarrow Bay

It seems inconceivable that over six miles of the most beautiful coast in England has been shut off and under the control of the War Department for nearly half a century. Cockpit Head, Mupe Bay, Arish Mell, Worbarrow, Gad Cliff and Brandy Bay lost their freedom because the area was convenient for a Royal Armoured Corps firing range. Bindon Hill, with its earth defences built in the 5th century BC and its little chapel erected by monks in the 13th century, has withstood the shells since 1916, and has grown more and more scarred as bigger and more sophisticated tanks have pumped their shells into the 560-foot-high chalk hill.

In 1974 the Government decided to give the public some restricted access. A committee of interested bodies made suggestions which resulted in the provision of Range Walks. Explorers *must* keep to the marked roads and tracks because about 70,000 armour-piercing shells are fired each year and some do not go off. Before the walks are opened each season, the area is searched for unexploded shells, but many remain undetected in the rough, away from the paths.

One of the most beautiful and easy-going walks is the route from the car park and picnic spot at Whiteway, on the steep hill from Creech Grange. The view from the path at Whiteway is breathtaking. In the distance, the great mass of Portland slumbers, and when the sun is low the Downs resemble giant waves rolling in from the Channel as if to wipe out Dorset. A path leads to Lawford Sheard, on the Dorset coastal ridgeway, and on to Flowers Barrow and Rings Hill. Part of this Iron Age hillfort, over 500 feet above sea level, collapsed over the cliffs in the 18th century. If you are energetic, you can return via Tyneham village, but if you do, remember there is a steep climb back to the car at Whiteway.

The explorer must on no account miss Tyneham. This once-proud little village, with a couple of terraces of houses, a school and a church near a Manor House, was taken over by the military in 1939. At the end of the Second World War there was a long fight to get it returned to the villagers, but the campaign failed. Slowly the village decayed, shells splintered the stonework and the weeds and brambles grew to hide the ruins. Today the Manor House has long gone, but the ruined cottages have been tidied up, the church of St Mary is still intact, though with its windows boarded up, and the school house has been restored as a museum. Despite this, Tyneham will never live again; the telephone kiosk - installed in the 1930s - still stands, but no one calls.

There is an excellent walk from Lulworth to Kimmeridge which takes about 4½ hours. From Lulworth Cove the Dorset Coast Path climbs up the cliff until it reaches the boundary fence of the Royal Armoured Corps Gunnery Range at 'Fossil Forest' gate. the path then follows the coastline past the Fossil Forest, where the fossilised tree stumps can be seen on the cliff (see Lulworth), to Mupe Bay where bathing is allowed. The path then ascends Bindon Hill, rising steeply to Cockpit Head and following the very narrow cliff edge before descending precipitously to Arish Mell. This part of the coast path is arduous and is not recommended for casual walkers. Arish Mell foreshore is a danger area and is closed to the public.

Continuing eastwards the path climbs steadily to the important Iron Age hillfort known as Flower's Barrow, where it meets the old Dorset coastal ridgeway. The coast path runs down into Tyneham Valley above Worbarrow Bay and its bathing beach. It then climbs up from Gold Down along the top of Gad Cliff, where some spectacular views reward the walker. Care should be taken along this stretch because the cliff edge is dangerous. Walkers are, moreover, particularly requested not to disturb the wildlife which abounds in this area. From Gad Cliff the coast path skirts round beneath Tyneham Cap before descending to the range boundary at Kimmeridge Gate beside the oil well.

# LULWORTH

Lulworth Cove is a beauty spot which belongs to the nation, a natural harbour scooped out of the romantic Purbeck coast. Whether the explorer energetically climbs the surrounding slopes to enjoy the breathtaking views, marvel at the chalk cliffs rising from the beach of this seapool, or becomes fascinated by the rising tide sweeping around the bay in concentric rings, he will become entranced by nature's maritime joke.

The cove is about a mile around its perimeter, formed at the foot of Bindon Hill by the sea breaking through the hard rock on the seaward side, to erode away the soft sediments behind into a circular bay. On the western side of the entrance, visitors can easily climb down a slope into Stair Hole, a roofless cavern formed in the same way as its larger neighbour, and see the weird shapes assumed by strata which were buckled and twisted millions of years ago. A little further west over the hilltop is another bay, where Durdle Door, a strange Portland stone archway, juts into the sea from the Purbeck cliff. It shelters a lovely bathing beach, but the climb down the cliff is hard work.

Lulworth's most treasured site is the fossil forest, to the east of the cove. Because it is within the army control, this can only be visited when the Range Walks are open - usually at weekends and throughout August. This may be a blessing because souvenir hunters in the past have taken much away. Almost before time began, this was a mighty forest. What remains, a mere half mile of it, are the tree stumps turned to stone, standing on the cliff midway between the sea and the clifftop. It is an awesome place to picnic and now very difficult to reach except from the sea.

When the explorer sits among these ancient relics, he should forget the modern world and try to imagine the strange creatures which once lived here, ten million years ago. As he munches into a crisp lettuce sandwich, he should think of the dinosaurs which roamed the land, browsing the on the primeval herbage and preying on one another, and the pterodactyls which soared overhead on their great wings.

Stair Hole

Eventually the forest, with its giant cyad trees and primitive pines, became buried beneath clay and freshwater limestone, which protected it until it was exposed again by erosion.

Lulworth has lost some of its magic now that the car makes access so simple, but there was a time when paddle steamers ran thir bows right on to the shore, and ladies in crinolines climbed down a sloping ramp to spend a while on the beach. This was the peaceful cove where Keats, in the autumn of 1820, sheltered from a storm on his way to Italy to die. Beneath these white cliffs he re-wrote his poem *Bright star, would I were steadfast as thou art.* By coincidence another poet, Rupert Brooke — who also loved this place — dropped his book of Keats' poems into the water and dived off his boat to rescue it, years later. Today only fishermen and a few adventurous yachtsmen sail through the narrow entrance.

West Lulworth, the nearby village of lovely thatch, has a welcoming old inn. Two miles inland is East Lulworth, on the edge of the army ranges and constantly disturbed by shellfire. Here, in a 640-acre park of beautiful trees, is Lulworth Castle. Gutted by fire in 1929, it is every schoolboy's idea of a castle: square with a round tower at each corner and a battlemented roof. It was built of stone from the ruins of Bindon Abbey, and the foundations were laid in the year of the Armada.

During the Civil War, the castle was held at different times by King and Parliament, but its six-foot thick walls never suffered from cannon fire. The Welds have been Lords of the Manor since 1641 and their Catholic church, built in 1792, can be seen from the village road. The first Roman Catholic Bishop of America was consecrated in this church. The village church is also in the castle grounds — St Andrew, rebuilt in Victorian times, but retaining its handsome medieval tower.

Lulworth Cove with (inset) Durdle Door

# WEYMOUTH AND PORTLAND

Sea Life Centre.
Weymouth
Nothe Fort.
North Ship Channel.
Breakwater
East Ship Channel
PORTLAND HARBOUR.
Breakwater
South Ship Channel.
Portland
THE FLEET
CHESIL BEACH
Bill of Portland

~~~ Breakwater.
.......... Coast Footpath.

# WEYMOUTH

Civil War cannon ball embedded in a wall in Maiden Street

The town that most people regard as Weymouth was originally Melcombe Regis. This includes the main shoping centre and seafront. The real Weymouth lies across the harbour on the Nothe side. Bitter battles were fought between the two until the reign of Elizabeth I, when they were amalgamated in 1571.

A cannon ball still embedded in the side of an old house in Maiden Street, near the Old Guildhall, is a battle scar of the Civil War. All the buildings in this block down to the Ship Inn on the quayside, date from the Tudor and Stuart periods.

In busy St Mary's Street, the sign of the Black Dog invites the thirsty to the town's oldest tavern, recorded during the Civil War as the scene of a brutal murder. At the harbour end of this street, the dominant Guildhall of 1836 is impressive, with an Ionic portico set above a rusticated arcade.

If you love ships, the harbour is absorbing. You can come within touching distance of cross-channel ferry boats, yachts, tugs, fishing boats and one of the country's largest lifeboats. This busy harbour, only a few hundred feet wide, is full of interest, with ancient inns and shops lining the quayside.

The Melcombe Regis shore has the Channel ferry boats at its seaward end, and the boat train slowly glides along the harbourside, nosing its way between cars and shore-parked yachts. The explorer can pass the time of day with the passengers on the train, and even shake their

The Jubilee Clock

Whether you approach Weymouth from the coastal road or descend from the hills out of Dorchester, you are soon aware that this little English resort clings tenaciously to its royal past. Hotels bear royal names and George III, who did a great public relations job for the town, is remembered by a fine statue, standing on a great plinth where the main shopping streets meet. He is guarded by a lion and a unicorn. The statue of Queen Victoria presents a back view to all arrivals, the Queen probably preferring the view of the famous sandy seafront.

In 1789 George III was persuaded to try sea bathing for his health. According to legend, when he submerged into the briny, a concealed band struck up the National Anthem. After that he regularly stayed at what is now the Gloucester Hotel. His presence attracted the wealthy and fashionable, and the resort grew rich on the proceeds. On a hillside above the bay at Preston, cut into the chalk, the king is portrayed riding a white charger.

The lovely bay, sometimes known as the Naples of England because of its blue water, has one of the safest bathing beaches in the country. The rows of Georgian-style terraces facing the sea were built in the late 18th and early 19th centuries, and the Jubilee Clock dominating the seafront commemorates the Golden Jubilee of Queen Victoria.

The Esplanade

Weymouth Harbour

hands as it moves so slowly. Believe it or not, a man walks in front of the engine with a red flag and holds up the traffic at the busy Westham bridge crossing, as officials have done ever since the line opened in 1880.

Beyond Town Bridge and up to the second bridge at Westham, the Wey is known as the Backwater. Today it is a place for mass mooring of pleasure craft, but it was once the way the Roman galleys came en route to Radipole, the original port higher up the river.

Radipole Lake nature reserve

Beyond Westham Bridge is the vast Radipole Lake, now a nature reserve and home of Weymouth's own swans. Here the water is fresh, and 80 pairs breed among the reeds. Vast numbers of birds nest in the reedbeds including the sedge warbler, the rare bearded tit, and the Cetti's warbler with its harsh song. In the autumn migrating birds use the lake as a refuelling base and in winter it becomes a wildfowl refuge.

The ill feeling between the two towns is long over, so you can retrace your steps and cross back into Weymouth over the Town Bridge. To the right is the 'old town', mostly flattened by a land mine during the last war, which destroyed a whole High Street of quaint buildings. But the Town Hall at the top end is still standing, built of the humblest stone. 16th-century in origin, it was largely rebuilt in 1774 and 1896. In its shadow is the Boot Inn, a pub of character where you expect to see swashbuckling pirates of the 17th century come swaggering through the doorway. It has five-light upper windows and lower windows with hood moulds and hollow chamfered mullions.

Return again to the bridge and walk down Trinity Road, past some of the town's oldest houses, and leave the harbour for a while to turn into Hope Square. The pleasant permanent odour of hops indicates that this is the home of the Devenish Brewery. A narrow lane leads up to the Nothe, with views of Portland harbour on one side and a view of Weymouth and the harbour on the other. At the tip of the Nothe is the Victorian fort built to protect Portland Harbour (see page   ). Climb down to sea level through wooded slopes and you have the choice: you can cross the harbour by one of the little ferry boats, rowed by old salts who will spin a yarn as you trail your fingers in the cool water, or walk back along Nothe Parade, past the yacht club and the magnificent Arun-type lifeboat moored outside the old lifeboat house — a relic of the days when Weymouth men rowed and sailed their lifeboat out into the storm.

The parish church of St Mary, in St Mary's Street, is surmounted by a giant clock. Inside it has a painting of the Last Supper by Sir James Thornhill, a Weymouth man whose greatest work was the decoration of the interior of the dome of St Paul's Cathedral, designed by Sir Christopher Wren. Both were Members of Parliament for Weymouth, and their portraits hang side by side in the Guildhall.

Sandsfoot Castle, a mile from the town centre and overlooking Portland Harbour, was a fortress built in 1541 to complement Portland Castle in the days when there were no breakwaters. Coastal erosion has destroyed much of Henry VIII's 'right goodly fortress'.

Two other buildings of historical interest are the 17th-century White Hart Inn in Lower Bond Street and the Old Rooms Inn at Trinity Street, of the same period, with its bold porch projecting out on to the pavement.

St Alban Street

The romantic make the four-mile journey out of town along the Dorchester Road to Upway, the source of the town's river. Here generations of ladies have dispensed cups of water from the spring, and commanded the drinkers to make a wish.

Weymouth is so dominated by Georgian and Victorian buildings that you are apt to forget the Roman connection. Where the coast road turns left at Lodmoor as you leave town, you should take the road which continues up the hillside. On the crest a sign directs you to the site of a Roman temple. Leave the car, and a walk of about 100 yards brings you to the site. Originally a Romano-British style square building, only the footings of the temple remain. Crude excavations in the 1800s destroyed the archaeological stratification which is now considered so important, but valuable finds included coins (AD 72 to AD 385), urns and spears.

# SEA LIFE CENTRE

Sea Life Centre open
daily from 9.00

Price guide C

Butterfly Farm open
daily 10.00 - dusk

You cannot call the Sea Life Centre at Lodmoor Country Park an aquarium — it is more of a unique underwater experience, where you can walk through a tunnel along the seabed, and see giant fish swimming around and over you. In the tunnel you are surrounded by over 36,000 gallons of water weighing nearly 200 tons. Shoals of mullet and sea bream swim by, and large tope and spurdog — sharks common in British waters — stare menacingly through the inch-thick plate glass.

The Sea Life Centre at Weymouth is the largest display of native marine life in Europe. Four separate habitat displays — shoreline, sand, cliff and ocean — show the fish in carefully reconstructed natural surroundings.

A close encounter with a thornback ray

Many of the specimens were caught locally. The Gulf Stream brings warm currents to the tip of Portland and some of the fish which were caught nearby are normally native to the Mediterranean. Some extraordinary fish have been brought to the centre, including a 45lb electric ray and an even bigger 50lb sting ray.

Much of the centre is housed in five hexagonal-shaped buildings, attractively clad in pine, each featuring a different marine habitat. The first of these is the most conventional, showing hundreds of shoreline species, many caught by local fishermen.

In tanks and conditions identical to those on a commercial fish farm, fish farming (aquaculture) techniques are demonstrated. Depending on the time of year, different species of fish are kept; the surrounding display explains the systems used. This display looks into the future development of marine aquaculture and its importance to the world fish catch.

The cliff habitat has a raised walkway to enable you to view the fish from above as well as seeing them eye to eye through the sides of the huge tank. The cliff has been modelled on Dorset's famous beauty spot, Durdle Door.

In the shoreline pavilion, conger eels peer out of rock holes and lobsters trundle by. In the cliff habitat, a sunken boat in the 26,000 gallons of water provides an exciting environment for the brightly coloured wrasse. It is very difficult to keep the local mackerel in captivity, because of the speed at which they swim, but because of the large size of the tank at Sea Life, a shoal of mackerel is now established.

Artificial rock pools have been created to hold the many types of creatures, both fish and invertebrates, that are found in our native rock pools. Visitors are able to pick up and examine these animals, and can study their habitat, physical characteristics, locomotion, feeding and behaviour. This concept has proved to be very popular with both teachers and pupils.

The 'Future of the Seas' is the first exhibition open to the public to explore in depth man's involvement with the oceans — the last major frontier on Earth. 71 per cent of the surface of the globe is covered by the oceans and this exhibition aims to bring attention to the uses and abuses to which the seas are subject, and emphasise the value of ocean resources in sustaining life on earth.

The exhibition includes several impressive features — a model of a North Sea oil rig, a mock-up of a ship's bridge and an audio-visual presentation. Perhaps the most exciting exhibit of all is the mini-submarine *Pisces III*, which is on loan from BUE Sub Sea, Edinburgh. This is the mini-sub that was involved in the deepest-ever manned rescue, in 1973 off the coast of Cork.

The Sea Life Centre is part of a country park complex which includes a model railway and a butterfly farm set in a wildflower meadow. The farm is laid out like a tropical rain forest where butterflies breed among exotic plants.

# THE NOTHE FORT AND BREAKWATER

The natural Nothe headland serves as a protective barrier between Weymouth and the English Channel storms, but the great Victorian fort at its tip is linked with the Portland Breakwater to form part of the 19th-century defences of the naval dockyard establishment. Now the property of Weymouth Corporation, the fort has been opened to give the public a chance to see how the Victorian soldiers lived in their gloomy barracks.

If you climb to the heights of Bincleaves near the Nothe you may be able to visualise the scene long before Portland had a harbour. There were no breakwaters, and only the Chesil Beach stood between the English Channel and Weymouth Bay. There must have been defences on the Nothe since the River Wey first became used for trade and commerce, but it was in 1625 that two pieces of ordnance were placed there on a platform of Purbeck stone at the expense of the Corporation. In 1644, the Parliamentary Admiral Lord Warwick ordered the Nothe headland to be fortified at government expense. It was the scene of considerable fighting in 1645 when Royalist forces attacked the Parliamentary garrison at Weymouth, and captured the Nothe - only to lose it a few days later. On March 3 1645, two Royalist plotters were hanged on the Nothe headland. There is a tradition that the cannon ball still set in the wall of a house in Maiden Street was lodged there during that battle, but there are other stories, and indeed it is so centrally and neatly placed that it could have been put there much later. After the Civil Wars, the fort was abandoned and the stonework sold.

The way in through the outer defences

For the first half of the 19th century, Weymouth was without a major coastal defence, and Portland Harbour depended for its safety on the ancient guns in Henry VIII's castle at Portland. But in 1857 approval was given for the construction of heavy batteries on the Nothe, and the fort we now know was started in 1860. The original contractor went bankrupt and the work was finished by Royal Engineers and convicts. The massive armament included two tiers of the heaviest rifled guns available, capable of throwing projectiles of 300lbs weight over three miles, and twelve guns in massive casements. In conjunction with another fort on one of the breakwaters, it provided a crossfire sufficient to prevent any enemy ships entering Portland Harbour. The fort had accommodation for 200 officers and men and a magazine for storing amunition deep in its bowels.

It is amusing to note that as early as 1859 the Mayor led a delegation to the war authorities complaining that the large fort had robbed people of their favourite open space.

The breakwater defences which form the great Portland Harbour were begun in 1850. To provide labour for the construction of the stone walls, which stand 12 feet above high water, a convict prison was established at Portland. 1500 men were engaged in the building of the four walls with their three entrances. The two sections nearest Boncleaves at Weymouth were completed in 1903.

In the First World War, the southern entrance was thought to be vulnerable to submarine attack and an old battleship, HMS *Hood*, was temporarily sunk across the entrance. Unfortunately she turned turtle and sank upside down; she is there to this day, and is said to be an excellent fishing ground.

Looking east from inside the Nothe Fort

During the 18th century a circular brick building was built to house two traversing guns, but they were removed in 1821 and the building was converted into a station for the Preventative Service, a predecessor of Trinity House.

# PORTLAND

Hardy called Portland the Gibraltar of Wessex. 'It stretches out like the head of a bird into the English Channel' he wrote, 'the towering rock, the houses above houses, one man's doorstep rising above his neighbour's chimney, the gardens hung up by one edge to the sky, the vegetables on apparently vertical planes, the unity of the whole island as a solid and single block of limestone, for centuries immemorial the home of a curious and almost distinctive people cherishing strange beliefs and singular customs'.

Four and a half miles long by two miles wide, with a circumference of nine miles, this solid mass of rock is linked to the Dorset mainland by the 18-mile long shingle bank of Chesil beach. It has ten villages or hamlets with Anglo-Saxon names. There are few trees and, until the decline in the stone trade, their place was taken by numerous stiff-legged derricks used for craning out the stone from the quarries, most of which are now dormant, and merely scars on the landscape. The road alongside the beach from Weymouth is the only way on to the island. It leads to The Square, a meeting place and departure point for all visitors, situated in the fishing village of Chiswell or Chesil. Parts of the village are built on the beach itself, and parts cling to the hillside. The occupants of those behind the beach live in constant fear of flooding from Channel storms.

A left-hand turn from The Square will take you past the helicopter port and lead into Castletown docks, and the entrance to the naval base and dockyard. Henry VIII's Portland Castle, unlike its crossfire partner Sandsfoot at Weymouth, is not a ruin and visitors are welcome. It has been restored as far as possible to its original state and represents a transitional type between a Middle Ages castle and a bastioned fort, and has a two-storied tower with wings for garrison quarters. The casement for the main battery occupies a seaward quadrant, with gun platforms on either side.

Retrace your steps to Fortuneswell, the shopping village on the hillside grouped around St John's Church, built in 1840. Beyond, the road divides — the right-hand fork leads to the heights of the island, nearly 500 feet above sea level, and the left turn leads to the Verne Citadel, a site inhabited in prehistoric and Roman times. The present fortress on this site, concealed by grass banks, was another link in the defence of Portland Harbour. You will not wish to enter because it is now an H.M. Prison Training Centre. Verne Common, by the Citadel Dyke, offers breathtaking views of the harbour and dockyard, while to the right are the sullen grey walls of the borstal, formerly a convict prison. The B3154, which is the motor road from the Fortuneswell divide, gives exquisite views of Chesil Beach — as far as Devon on a clear day.

Before driving into Easton, turn left by the football ground for a closer view of the drab borstal buildings at The Grove. Stop on the road to see St Peter's church. Built in 1872 by convict labour, it is now the Borstal Chapel. It has a roof

The lighthouse at Portland Bill, and Pulpit Rock

fashioned with timber brought from Riga on the Baltic coast. The pulpit, lectern and font were cut in stone by Irish Fenians and Whitechapel thieves, and the illumination around the windows was the work of a convict who served sentences under three different names. The mosaic in the chancel was laid by 15-year old Constance Kent, serving a life sentence for murdering her stepbrother. The convict settlement became a borstal in 1921 and one of the schemes carried out by the boys over the decades was the clearing and levelling of an old quarry to create one of the finest sports arenas in the south.

Pennsylvania Castle Hotel

Easton is grouped around its little park, but the explorer will quickly pass through to Wakeham which has more to offer. Here, on a bend in the road, is a row of typical Portland stone cottages with Avice's Cottage at its end. Mentioned in Hardy's *The Well Beloved*, it is now part of the Portland Museum.

Across the road, a bramble-covered patch is passed unnoticed by most travellers. From a little quarry there, long since disused, came the stone for the Cenotaph in Whitehall. Also on this bend is Pennsylvania Castle Hotel, a cliff-edge mansion built in the 19th century for a former Governor of the island, and the ruin of Rufus Castle — locally known as Bow and Arrow Castle. It was beseiged and captured by Robert, Earl of Gloucester in 1142. Through an archway, the explorer can descend steps to Church Ope Cove, a favourite beach picnic spot.

Back on the road, it is all downhill past quarries on one side and the picnic spots on the Southwell landslip on the other, until the Bill of Portland comes down almost to sea level, and the towering red and white lighthouse dominates the scene, making the original light — now a residence — look insignificant. Around the lighthouse is a vast car park and tired old wooden huts from which teas and lobster lunches have been served for generations.

Clamber over discarded squares of stone beside old quarries and you will see the strangest of rock tables. Pulpit Rock defies the full force of the south-westerly gales, but on a good day toe holds assist you to the top. Through the

generations numerous sailing ships, yachts and even a paddle steamer have come to grief at its base, and the island's west coast from here back to Chiswell has a long history of shipwreck. Deadman's Bay is a graveyard for countless ships.

On the beach at Chiswell in summer the mackerel shoals are netted using the specially designed lerret boats, and visitors can make a purchase straight from the beach.

Before Inigo Jones discovered the value of Portland stone in the 17th century, and a new-look London grew up as ton after ton of it was quarried by hand for such edifices as the Banqueting Hall of Whitehall Palace and, later, the new St Paul's Cathedral, the island's main living was the rearing of sheep. The local tan-faced variety provided the famous Portland mutton; the breed is now almost extinct, but a few can be seen in the grounds of Portland Museum.

Portlanders are a close community and the families are much intermarried. Families such as the Pierces, Whites, Elliots and Combens worked the quarries for generations and seldom accepted strangers. Even now, visitors may be treated with suspicion. Today the stone is quarried with the aid of modern technology; the romance has gone but the stone remains the same.

When the great ships of the line — *Rodney, Nelson, Repulse, Renown, King George V*, and many other fine battle craft — moored in the harbour before the last war, it was the custom to come and see the ceremony of sunset from Portland Heights and Bincleaves at Weymouth. When the crimson sun sank below the western horizon, the Ensigns were slowly lowered and the bugle notes echoed across the still waters. A cherished memory for some, and it will never be seen again.

The little railway which conveyed passengers and stone from Portland Heights, crawling around the cliff sides into Weymouth, has also long gone — one of Beeching's cruellest cuts.

This bare stony peninsula cannot be called beautiful, yet it has an appeal which draws you to its historic shores. On a hot summer's day, you might be on a Mediterranean isle, but it is more exciting when stormy seas thud against the beach and roar over the pebbles. On rare occasions Portland is cut off by seas built up by wind and tide, and becomes a true island for a few dramatic hours.

A group of Portland cottages

## *Introducing*
# New Styles and Services to the Channel Islands for 1985

**Portsmouth Service**
Luxury travel by 'Starliner' service to the Channel Islands
— **commencing 31 March.**

**Weymouth Service**
'Sunliner' service, travel is by day sailing in either direction
— **commencing 31 March.**

Travel Sealink to the
CHANNEL ISLANDS '85
Introducing Sealink's New Sunliner and Starliner Services

EARL GODWIN

Fares and Timetables to Guernsey and Jersey

SEALINK BRITISH FERRIES
*Determined to give you a better service*

Advance information brochures with service schedules, fares and booking forms for the Channel Islands from both ports will be available in November.

Make sure you have a copy of your brochure by sending to:
**SEALINK UK LTD, FREEPOST, SOUTHAMPTON SO9 1BH**

SEALINK **BRITISH FERRIES**

# WEYMOUTH AND PORTLAND MUSEUMS

Weymouth Museum open
Tue-Sat 10.00-1.00,
2.00-5.00
Price guide A

Portland Museum open
Winter Tue-Sat 10.00-1.00,
2.00-5.00
Summer Tue-Fri 10.00-1.00,
2.00-5.00; Sat-Sun
1.00-5.00
Price guide A

Lerret mackerel boat

A former school on the Backwater shore at Westham Bridge houses Weymouth Museum, which features the history and archaeology of Weymouth and the surrounding area.

As expected, pride of place — in fact a whole room — is devoted to the bathing machine which King George III used for his dips at Weymouth. For many years between the wars it stood at the bottom of a garden overlooking Newtons Cove on the Nothe, its coat-of-arms faded, serving as a summer house. Now proudly presented in the museum in glistening white paint, it has wheels of the type used in its working days, and its coat-of-arms has been restored.

Among the Tudor relics is a treasure chest which formed part of the baggage of Philip and Joan of Castile when they were stormbound at Weymouth in 1506. She was the princess who put on her finest dress and all her jewellery when she thought their ship would be wrecked in Weymouth Bay. Another great treasure chest in the collection was brought ashore from the captured Armada galleon *San Salvador,* brought into Weymouth as a prize.

Weymouth Priory was closed down in 1538 but amongst its relics is a Prior's Chair. An inscription on it states that it has the magical power of granting a direct passage to heaven to anyone who should die whilst sitting on it. An amusing notice says 'We regret that we are unable to grant this facility to visitors as the chair is old and weak, and we too are subject to the Trades Description Act'.

Much of the town's history is presented pictorially. A coat of arms of George I, painted by Sir James Thornhill, and many other paintings and drawings of the period between 1789 and 1805 are on show. In 1790 John Love, who weighed 26 stone, published a series of prints of Weymouth, and Henry Burn painted the scene as the Albion Balloon ascended from Weymouth Race Course in 1842, taking Mr Green and Captain Currie on a trip which ended at Bere Regis. Other pictures recall the Market House which was next to St Mary's Church, and demolished in 1939.

The old fire engine

An 18th-century fire engine is prominently displayed, and a lerret mackerel boat is of interest to boat and fishing enthusiasts. The lerret was specially designed for fishing off the treacherous Chesil Beach, and few of them still exist.

Weymouth was once the home port of the Cosens and Co. paddle steamer fleet, well known all along the south coast. Two of the ships, the *Victoria* and *Empress,* used to beach at Lulworth Cove, so paddle steamer bygones have an important place in the display.

The Portland Museum is housed in a building made famous by Thomas Hardy, at Wakeham on the top of Portland on the road that leads to the Bill. Avice's Cottage, featured in Hardy's *The Well Beloved,* stands at the end of a picturesque row of Portland stone cottages at the entrance to Church Ope Cove. Now enlarged, the museum is mainly housed in Wakeham Cottage, behind Avice's Cottage which is now the home of temporary collections. Stone and fossils are on display together with convict, marine and smuggling relics but, strangely, the most interesting items are living. Portland sheep, now very rare, graze in the garden.

King George III's bathing machine

# ABBOTSBURY AND THE FLEET

# CHESIL BEACH

The beach sweeps west from Portland for 18 miles

The old fishermen waiting by their boats for a sign of mackerel will tell visitors that Chesil Beach is the Eight Wonder of the World and that it appeared overnight. The beach of pebbles is 18 miles long, and stretches from the Isle of Portland to Bridport, connecting the island to the mainland and sheltering Weymouth from the Channel gales. 50 to 60 feet above sea level at its highest, and about 200 yards wide, it is one of the longest beaches in Europe. It can be viewed in its entirety from the top of Portland. Visitors can reach it at several points but the Fleet Water, which runs between it and the mainland for eight miles from Wyke to Abbotsbury, forms a barrier to access. The most popular place to start a walk is between Ferrybridge and Portland. There are bus stops and ample parking here, but the walking itself is arduous because the pebbles are at their largest on this stretch. Chesil is a Saxon word meaning shingle.

The beach has a terrifying history of shipwreck. Wyke church graveyard is full of sailors and soldiers who perished on the beaches, and thousands more have been buried in the pebbles. One of the worst disasters occurred on November 18 1795, when the transport ships *Venus, Piedmont* and *Catherine* were lost off Wyke the same day.

For many generations the fishermen along this coast have netted the famous Portland mackerel. Traditionally they use special boats called lerrets, built to overcome the powerful surf which thunders ashore. They got their name from one of the first boats which was called *Lady of Loreto,* owned by a fisherman who had seen a church of that dedication in his travels. Although they have been used for 200 years only a few are seen on the beach today, but there is a lerret on display in Weymouth Museum.

Wire baskets packed with beach pebbles protect the village of Chiswell from the sea

It must be stressed that bathing from the beach, except where notices give permission, is extremely dangerous. There is a sharp dip in the shingle and a very strong undertow.

The Dorset Coast Path runs along the shoreward side of the Fleet, and the beach 'comes ashore' at Abbotsbury near the swannery and continues along the foot of the cliffs and downs past Bexington and Burton Bradstock to Bridport.

The pebbles consist chiefly of a white calcareous kind mixed with jaspers and quartz. In the main they have been carried by storm waves and currents from a submerged beach off Bridport, and some have been washed direct from the Dorset and Devon coasts.

At Portland, where pebbles first come ashore, they are largest and least rounded, but as the storm waves and ocean pressures and currents drive them along the beach to the west, they gradually become smaller and more rounded. Over the years pebbles weighing more than ten pounds can be reduced to small stones weighing mere ounces. At Bridport it is almost gravel. It is said that if fishermen get driven ashore in foggy weather, they can locate their position by the size of the pebbles.

# THE FLEET

The Fleet is a sheltered lagoon 7¾ miles long which opens to the sea at Ferrybridge. Chesil Beach forms its seaward shore and along the irregular land coast the waters wash the shores of Wyke Regis, Fleet and Langton Herring. Fleet was the model for the village in the novel *Moonfleet,* a tale of smuggling written in 1898 by Meade Faulkner. A hotel which bears the name Moonfleet was originally Fleet House, built in 1603 for the Mohun family who inhabited it between the 16th and 18th centuries.

East Fleet was practically wiped out in the great gale of 1824, and the church was swept away leaving only the chancel, which still remains. During that gale the sloop *Ebenezer* was swept up on to the top of Chesil bank and relaunched into the Fleet.

Renowned for its wildlife, the head of the Fleet forms the inland bay which is the home of the famous Abbotsbury swans. Other interesting birds which can be seen in Fleet waters are reed warblers, firecrests, terns, shelducks, herons, reed buntings, cormorants and great crested grebes.

# HARDY'S MONUMENT

The monument

When the explorer arrives at the Hardy's Monument, a landmark 780 feet up on the crest of Blackdown Hill which separates Weymouth from Dorchester, he is at a spot to which many Weymouth people have never ventured, although they see the monument almost every day of their lives. Many wrongly believe that it commemorates Thomas Hardy the author, but this very Victorian 70-foot octagonal stone tower is in fact a memorial to Sir Thomas Masterman Hardy, the naval officer in whose arms Nelson is reputed to have died.

It was erected in 1884 to a design by Arthur Dyke Ackland-Troyte. Crinoline-like base mountings support the tower which has a bulging top. The door is locked and no-one is allowed to climb to the top. It matters not because the hill itself offers panoramic views which, on a clear day, include the Isle of Wight and Start Point in Devon. Weymouth lies to the south and the Isle of Portland looks like a slumbering whale in the background. Looking inland, you see rich Dorset farmland with the valley of the Frome in the foreground.

A wonderful picnic spot, it is best approached via the B3159 from Upwey to Winterborne Abbas, turning left just beyond Martinstown on to the road marked 'To Hardy's Monument'; this climbs across the heathland to the site, which is now in the safe keeping of the National Trust. There is an interesting stone seat at the foot of the monument, a memorial to another warrior. Sit awhile and spare a thought for Lt. Col. Digby Oswald DSO, who died on the Somme in 1916 during the first Great War.

The young Hardy was brought up in Portesham, two miles down the slopes of Blackdown. Born in 1760, he first went to sea at the age of twelve. After twelve months, he came ashore for three years schooling, then secretly went back to sea in the Merchant Navy. Later, in the Royal Navy, he became a Lieutenant at the age of 21 years. After a distinguished career, he became Nelson's Flag Captain and stayed at his side until that tragic day at Trafalgar. 'God bless you Hardy' were Nelson's last words.

Hardy ended his career as Governor of Greenwich Hospital. He always loved his 'Possum', as he called Portesham. His home, a plain building of two storeys, is in the village. In a garden across the road from it is a sundial brought from Kingston Russell where Hardy was born. It commemorates his father, Joseph Hardy. Masterman Hardy adored everything which came from Dorset, especially mutton, cheese and beer. Dorset beer, he said, was 'the best ever drunk'.

Back on Blackdown Hill, there are monuments much older than Hardy's. One mile south-west of the monument is the Hellstone. To reach it, follow the bridle path to Portesham which starts 200 yards past the memorial tower. Proceed down the path through the wood, and at Blackdown barn, a derelict farmhouse, keep right through a gate, turn left and climb the hill.

The Hellstone is a Neolithic dolmen which was incorrectly rebuilt in 1866, standing at the entrance to a chambered long barrow 88 feet long. The Hellstone is at the south-east end. It originally consisted of nine stone columns six feet high surmounted by a table ten feet by six feet erected in about 4000 BC. The barrow, like most others, is on high ground and was originally covered with earth before centuries of wind and rain washed the covering away exposing the stonework. The bones of the dead were placed inside.

If you enjoy these ancient stones, continue from Hardy's Monument towards Abbotsbury. A mile past the Portesham crossroads is Gorwell Farm. The Valley of the Stones is on the right, and the Grey Mare and Colts to the left, all that is left of a long barrow.

The Hellstone

# ABBOTSBURY

The village, and a view from near St Catherine's Chapel

Abbotsbury, a showpiece village, welcomes explorers to its peaceful streets where predominantly yellow stone buildings create a warm and mellow atmosphere when the sun shines. The home of early monks, it later saw bloodshed and violence during the Civil War. One of its main attractions is the famous swannery, first established by the monks to provide birds for their table.

Nine centuries ago the brave Orc, a senior member of Canute's household, built an abbey at this coastal village. The monks swarmed in from Cerne and soon dominated the area. The abbey flourished for 500 years until the monasteries were dissolved during the reign of Henry VIII. Then the land passed to Sir Giles Strangways and, from the ruins, he built a mansion.

During the Civil War the mansion and church were garrisoned for the King, but the Parliament men stormed the buildings and bullet holes in the pulpit are claimed to have been made during the battle in 1644. In 1930, church restorers found two bullets embedded in a roof beam. In the heat of the battle the mansion blew up, killing all within it. Only an archway is left standing, although many stones have found their way into house walls in the village. The explorer will see the abbey area if he turns left when arriving in the village from the east.

Opposite the site is a charming manor house of a century earlier which has an external stone staircase, while south of the church and abbey, and beyond a peaceful pond where ducks play, is the tithe barn — Abbotsbury's pride and joy. It stands with the dignity of a cathedral, 272 feet long and 32 feet across, with closely-set buttresses and two porches. The roof is now partly thatched but originally would have been covered by stone slabs. It has been there since the 15th century.

Part of the tithe barn

The main street is attractive with raised pavements. Where the road bends, it forms a wide village centre with a typical Victorian schoolhouse facing the dignified Ilchester Arms Hotel. This hostelry could be as early as 1768.

Most explorers will wish to climb the 250-foot hill on which St Catherine's Chapel stands. This is a very substantial building, about 50 feet long with thick walls and mighty buttresses. It was built by the monks in the 14th century, probably as a mariners' chapel — a landmark for seamen. From the hilltop there is a magnificent view of Portland and the Channel. It can be reached by taking a left-hand turn beyond the Ilchester Arms. The lands still belong to descendants of Strangways via Horners, Fox-Strangways and the Earls of Ilchester.

Abbotsbury Castle is 1½ miles north-west of the village, a 20-acre hillfort on the summit of Wears Hill. It has not been excavated but there is probably a Roman fort in the west angle. Once occupied by the Durotriges tribe, its form is almost square, with ditches and ramparts. Stores of sling stones have been found at the spot.

St Catherine's Chapel

# ABBOTSBURY SWANNERY

Open daily mid-May to mid-Sept, 9.30-4.30 (no dogs)
Price guide B

The swans were introduced to Abbotsbury by the Benedictine monks who created a monastery there in the 11th century, but the earliest surviving record of numbers dates to 1591 when there were 410 swans and 90 cygnets. The flock was maintained by the monks as a source of fresh meat.

It is remarkable that this colony of mute swans has survived to the present day — there is no other colony of managed swans in the world. Its survival has depended on the protection of the Fox-Strangways family and the Earls of Ilchester, who have held the Abbotsbury Estate and the Fleet since the Dissolution of the Monasteries by Henry VIII. The management of the swans has altered little since medieval times.

The swannery is reached by following the road past the church and barn, where pedestrians take the shady road which descends sharply to the right and walk along a lane, through a gate on the right, and across two fields to a large door in a wall. Motorists continue on the top road to the car park and then take the same route.

There are now over 500 swans in the colony, and new cygnets hatch every year, taking 18 months to become fully decked in their white plumage.

The best time to visit the swannery is during nesting time. On a meadow formed at the head of the Fleet, the swans assemble to claim sites for nests where they will hatch their broods. The land around is lush, with pampas grass and fields as soft as a pile carpet. The birds stake their claims and set up nests, about 300 in a space of two acres. The best places are taken early by the older birds.

A feature of the swannery is the flight of the birds. The swans are not pinioned and are completely wild. When a number rise from the water on take-off, the noise of their thrashing wings is like an old paddle steamer.

The continued existence of the swannery is not entirely due to the protection afforded by the owners or their swanherd. The Fleet provides a marvellous habitat for the birds which, once the cygnets are fledged, gradually work their way eastwards in search of their main plant food, eelgrass *(Zostera marina)*, which covers the bed of the Fleet. The swannery has to close once the birds begin their move as the nesting area is deserted. It is this factor coupled with the scouring of the area by high water during the winter that ensures there is always a clean, disease-free nesting site available each spring.

# DUCK DECOY & REED BED

Most explorers will find the duck decoy and reed beds of interest. The decoy would originally have had four 'pipes' or netted tunnels into which the ducks were lured, to allow the decoy-man and his dogs to 'work' the decoy in most wind conditions. Ducks have well-developed senses of smell and hearing, thus great stealth is required to trap them. Today the decoy can only be worked after the swannery has been closed to the public in winter, and conditions are suitable to stalk the ducks feeding on corn spread in the pipes.

Abbotsbury forms one of a chain of bird-ringing stations and the records of the birds ringed here are sent to the British Museum. Rings have been returned to the Museum from as far afield as Siberia.

The reed here is *Phragmites australis* and it not only forms a valuable habitat for birds and insects, but also provides an excellent material for roofing. Until the 19th century, apart from some stone tile, reed thatch was the predominant roofing material locally. Today Abbotsbury cottages are still thatched with Abbotsbury reed and the tithe barn is still used to store it.

# ABBOTSBURY SUB-TROPICAL GARDENS

Open mid-March to
mid-Oct, 10.00-5.00
Price guide B

A short distance west of Abbotsbury village are the Sub-tropical Gardens, protected from the worst of the British weather by the sheltered nature of the valley in which they lie and their nearness to the waters of Lyme Bay. They are unique among British gardens, but the term sub-tropical is not quite accurate as the climate of the gardens falls between warm temperate and cool temperate.

The gardens have provided a home for unusual and tender plants for over 200 years since the Fox-Strangways made the first walled enclosure of just over an acre. With various members of the family adding new areas, the gardens now cover twenty acres.

Formality has never been considered in the layout of these beautiful gardens. Instead, an attempt has been made to paint a continually changing picture of the wild woodlands of the world.

The soil is deep, acid loam for the most part, only becoming shallow to the north where it overlies an outcrop of iron ore. The combination of soil type and climate allows lime-hating plants to thrive wonderfully, even though the surrounding countryside is predominantly of chalk and limestone. Thus, huge magnolias and tree rhododendrons accompany some of the largest and oldest camellias in cultivation, providing a splendid backdrop of spring colour against which other, more tender plants can produce their more subtle tones.

Roses are represented in the gardens by species roses and by old-fashioned shrub roses - about 200 kinds in all. June is the month to see these, when the great majority of trees and shrubs seem to take a summer holiday.

The Sino-British expedition to China in 1980 brought back more young plant specimens which were planted in a new extension of the gardens. This added acreage has also made it possible to accommodate the national reference collection of eucalyptus, as well as the national collection of salvia.

Some of the most important plants in the gardens were introduced to cultivation by the fourth Earl of Ilchester, William Fox-Strangways (after whom the genus *Stranvaesia* is named), including the holly-like *Villaresia muncronata* from Chile, which is now considered an endangered species in the wild.

Those who love plant life will be able to spend a whole day wandering around these acres, and enjoy the valley garden, the round garden and the walled garden, among many others, and see the forest tree sized *Picconia Excelsas* (a relative of the olive). These trees are the only ones of this size in the British Isles.

The explorer can buy plants, have tea and even bring the dog if he will stay on his lead. There is something flowering in this paradise nearly every month of the year, but the gardens are only open from the middle of March until mid-October.

# BRIDPORT AND LYME REGIS

# BRIDPORT

Castle Museum open daily
throughout the year
10.30 - 1.00; also
2.30-4.30 June-Sept
Price guide A

Museum of vintage cars
open Mon-Sat April-Sept
10.00-5.00
Price guide B

Bredy Farm Museum open
weekdays Whitsun-Sept,
milking 3.00-4.00 (no dogs)

If you think that history is about battles and kings, you will not find Bridport a historic town, although it was caught up in the Civil War and Monmouth's rebellion in 1685, and lofty earthworks on surrounding hills bear silent witness to prehistoric and Roman occupation. Bridport's true history concerns people, and their expertise in creating two commodities which have become world famous, and essential to sailors and fishermen — rope and netting. What started as a cottage industry before the days of King John, when hemp fields flourished in the district and rope and cordage were produced by locals, has grown into the largest net making business in Europe. Bridport nets are employed by fleets all over the world, and used extensively in sport and industry.

It was the growing of hemp *(Cannabis sativa)* in the alluvial river valleys, a practice introduced by the Romans, that formed the background to Bridport rope making. The first records of the trade appear in a sheriff's account book dated 1211, which mentions the sale of rope, yarn and sailcloth.

The fibre had to be spun into yarn, and to do this the men wrapped the hemp fibre around their waists, fixed one end to a rotating hook, and walked backwards paying out the fibre as they went. The effect of the revolving hook was to twist the fibres together into a simple yarn. To make the rope, a revolving hook twisted yarns, which were secured by a fixed hook at the other end.

The town, laid out like a letter T, bears many signs of this ancient craft. The long alleys stretching back from the wide main streets, built for making ropes and twines, can still be found. The revolving hook was turned by a crank handle on a frame known as the 'jack', which stood on the pavement at the end of the alley. The son of the family turned the jack and father walked up and down the alley paying out the hemp fibre. The wide pavements, it seems, had nothing to do with the rope walks, but they serve well for the market stands which open every Wednesday and Saturday in all main streets.

Henry VII decreed that all hemp grown within five miles of Bridport was to be reserved for his navy, and in Henry VIII's time the rope was used to secure naval cannon. It was also used to make the 'Bridport Dagger' a name which is presumed to have originated in the gaols of the time, since the term 'stabbed with a Bridport Dagger' meant hanging. It was the hangman's noose.

Samuel Gundry set up a rope and net making firm in 1665 and the name is still incorporated in the firm's present title, Bridport-Gundry. The town which once supplied hemp ropes for King John's fleet now supplies Queen Elizabeth II with nets of artificial fibre to catch jet fighters when they overshoot the runway. The explorer will learn more about the famous trade as he walks around the town, but the net making factory itself does not entertain visitors.

The Chantry House

The parish church of St Mary

East and West Street, part of the A35 through road, form the top of the T-shaped town layout. East Street is known for many interesting inns. The Greyhound can be traced back to 1300, and The Bull is of similar vintage. Another surviving old inn, The King of Russia, changed its name to King of the Belgians in the First World War and became the Lord Nelson during the second. From the end of the street, proceed half a mile along East Road to Lee Lane and you will see the stone commemorating the future King Charles II's flight from the town in disguise in 1651.

South Street is the oldest and most interesting thoroughfare, and runs south towards the sea from the Town Hall junction. Before 1261, the Town Hall site was an open marketplace. Then the White Friars came and built the chapel of St Andrew, which served the local merchants. After the Reformation it fell into disuse, but the tower was retained because it had a clock. In 1786 the present building was erected as a marketplace with Council Chamber and Courthouse built above it. Later, the magnificent clock tower was added and the market closed, the arched entrances being bricked up.

The museum and art gallery

As you progress south, observe the classical facade of the Arts Society, and some of the town's oldest houses. On the left is the elegant museum - obviously very old. The frontage is 16-century with a projecting five-sided porch. The Castle, as the building is called, may have taken its name from a small castle which existed on the site in about 1150, but it is more likely that it was an inn with that name, long before it became a museum.

The museum contains a great variety of items of local interest and history, which are illuminated by a restful light from the exquisite mullioned windows. Exhibits include flora, fauna and geology — with special emphasis on fossils found between Bridport and Lyme. The Roman occupation is represented by cavalry equipment and domestic ware. There is a fabulous doll collection dating from the end of the last century. Other bygones range from old farming machinery to ration books and mementos of the last war. But pride of place goes to one of two surviving net-making machines of the 1830's, and the replica of a 'Bridport Dagger' in the form of a gallows!

South Street has suffered from several major fires. In 1780, eighty townsmen were recruited to fight a particularly serious one. The fires are the reason for the strange mixture of building styles. The parish church of St Mary, of the 14th and 15th centuries, is on the site of an older building. Nearby are the almshouses dating from the 15th and 16th centuries. The Chantry House is the town's most interesting building; it appears that it was originally built as a lighthouse in the 13th century. Later it was added to and became the home of a priest. On the south wall is the cresset stand, the iron basket which held the primitive harbour light — a unique survival. Nearer the sea, the old brewery still operates its ancient Bridport-made iron water wheel today, but purely for effect. It can be seen from the road, but the brewery is not open to visitors.

In Foundry Lane, there is a museum of vintage cars and relics of a bygone age. Cars dating back to 1923, fire engines and steam rollers are featured.

Six miles from Bridport, between Burton Bradstock and Litton Cheney, is the Bredy Farm museum, with its collection of old farming implements.

Agricultural display in Bridport Museum

# WEST BAY

This is really Bridport Harbour, and the name West Bay can only have been thought up with the intention of creating a resort image. It lies snugly in a gap in the cliffs where the river Brit reaches the sea. There was a harbour here in the Middle Ages, but silting and the westward drift of the shingle makes it difficult to maintain a harbour at all. Only 1½ miles from Bridport, with a bus service, it is easily walked to by a field path starting behind St Mary's church.

The coastline has changed so much that it is difficult to know how ships, at one time, came almost to Bridport. When Daniel Defoe visited the place in 1722, there was no harbour, and fishermen operated from the continuous shingle beach, selling mackerel from their boats. In the 1740s a cut was made in the beach, two piers were constructed, and a novel way of preventing silting was devised. Gates were built across the Brit to hold back the water. When sufficient water had been amassed, the flood was released and it as it rushed out through the harbour entrance it scoured out the silt. The harbour faces the full force of the Channel storms and can only be entered in certain conditions. Few commercial boats call except the occasional coaster bringing in a load of wood, but the little square harbour is a base for fishing boats and yachts.

Shipbuilding has played an important part in the economy of West Bay, starting in the late 18th century. Nicholas Bools and his nephew, William Good, built 16 naval vessels between 1805 and 1814 at a shipyard west of the harbour. Later, bigger boats were built by the Cox family, mainly schooners, the largest being the *Speedy* of 1500 tons, launched in 1853. She was to be used on the Australian run to compete with the American clippers. The last vessel to be built there was launched in 1879.

Today boatbuilding is carried out factory-fashion at inland Bridport where the successful firm of Newbridge Boats build yachts in the 20-foot range. Their yard is the former New Zealand Rope works in Church Street.

In the 19th century the authorities turned their thoughts to the holiday trade. An esplanade was opened in 1887 and a small golf course was established on the east cliff. The old shipyard disappeared, first to be covered with chalets and, later, by more substantial buildings including flats and a shopping precinct. The house of the harbour controller became the Bridport Arms.

The golf course on the cliffs at West Bay offers the golfer not only a game in bracing sea air, but also some of the finest views of any club in the south. The 5,300-yard course, 200 feet above Chesil Beach, gives superb views of Portland and across Lyme Bay to the Devon coastline.

The harbour at low tide

# THE FOSSIL COAST

Another favoured walk is between Lyme and Charmouth, a distance of about two miles. This route passes under Black Ven (400 feet) where Lyme's most famous fossil was unearthed by eleven-year-old Mary Anning in 1810. With the help of her brother, she dug out a 35-foot specimen of ichthyosaurus — a dolphin-like reptile — which

Seatown, looking west along the fossil coast towards Golden Cap

Visitors come from all over the world to dig for fossils in the West Dorset cliffs, and Lyme Regis and its immediate vicinity is famous for its unusually rich fossil deposits. The six miles of coast from Pinhay Bay, which is just over the Devon border, to Seatown in the eastern direction, has produced many important fossils. The area has been prone to landslides, the biggest being the Great Landslip of Christmas Day 1839 after which, by the night of December 27, there was a chasm three-quarters of a mile long by 400 feet wide, and about a hundred feet deep. It forced up a reef parallel with the coast, covered in marine plants and shellfish, but it quickly subsided. Further slips took place in 1840 and 1911, and one in 1968.

The coastal footpath runs through the area of the Great Landslip, and keen walkers can journey the eight miles to Seaton in Devon, but the mile walk from the Cobb to Pinhay Bay is sufficient for most. Explorers are warned of the crumbly nature of the cliffs and the fact that undergrowth covers parts of the path. Leave the car at the car park by the Coram Tower at the junction of Cobb Road and Pound Street.

At beach level during this westerly walk, you will find a number of large fossil ammonites, extinct molluscs which resembled cuttlefish, but with shells curled up like a watch spring. Most of these fossils are embedded in the rock, and impossible to extract.

can now be seen in the Natural History Museum at South Kensington. Schoolchildren have been hacking at the cliffs ever since, hoping to make a similar find.

Mary eventually became one of the first professional fossil collectors, and went on to discover an articulated plesiosaurus skeleton and, in 1823, the first British fossil pterodactyl.

# GOLDEN CAP

Golden Cap is the highest clifftop on the south coast and one of the most lovely promontories. Crowned with a stratum of orange sandstone, which gives it its name, it is 619 feet above sea level. There are several routes leading to the top. One way is to leave the A35 at Chideock where a road leads to Seatown on the coast. Here, in the Anchor Inn almost on the beach, you can fortify yourself for the slow climb up the cliffs to reach the Cap's summit about a mile away. Some explorers may prefer to approach from the village of Morcombelake where the Dorset Knob biscuits are made. The road branches off the A35, passes Chardown Hill and brings you to the foot of Golden Cap. Whichever way you come, the final climb will reward you with views of Chesil and Portland to the west, and Lyme to the east.

# DORSET KNOBS

Open Mon-Fri 9.00-5.00

Thomas Hardy enjoyed them in the evening with Dorset's famous blue vinny cheese, and the old-time farm labourers dunked them in their early morning tea — a traditional start to the day. They were eating the Dorset knob, that shapeless biscuit guaranteed to destroy eating etiquette at any vicarage tea party because, on contact with a knife, it explodes into many small pieces.

The Moores began making Dorset knobs about 130 years ago at Stoke Mills in the Marshwood Vale, west Dorset, and it has always remained a family concern. If you ring them at their Morcombelake factory today, it is most likely that a Moores will answer the phone.

It all began when Samuel Moores married Eleanor some time before 1860 and, in between running a mill, farming and baking, reared eleven children. The farm in the vale was isolated and, in this rural setting, they sowed and harvested wheat, milled flour and baked bread in a small oven heated by faggots. When the baking was finished, it was the custom to make Dorset knobs by adding butter and sugar to the dough and rolling it out by hand into small buns. The dying heat of the oven was used to dry them out like rusks, and they probably took their name from the Dorset knob buttons which were still being made in the 19th century.

Seven sons of the marriage grew up and moved away, four of them to America where Harry continued the Dorset knob tradition. Samuel, the second son, established himself in Morcombelake in 1880 as a baker and continued making the Dorset knobs there. A staunchly religious Victorian, he married Frances, a governess at the nearby vicarage, and their six children were brought up 'with an iron discipline'. The bakery grew up around the house and the staff increased until after the First World War there were 13 bakers. They worked long hours, starting at dawn with only a break for prayers during the morning. In the 1920s the business expanded even more, and among the new staff was Abigail Larcombe, famous for her light sponge cakes. In 1924 Sam retired and his sons, Reg and Donald took over.

At this time water was still drawn from a well by hand, and the Moores were the first in the village to generate electricity. Labour was always found among the close-knit community. The chief confectioner in the 1920s was landlord of the Five Bells at Whitchurch, and the bakery foreman was landlord of the Sun Inn across the road.

There was sad decline in business during the Second World War and, on the deaths of Reg and Donald, the business was taken over by their sons Keith and Ivor. They rebuilt the trade, dropping the making of bread and cakes and concentrating on the unique Dorset knobs and sweet biscuits. When Ivor retired, Keith was joined by his wife, Gill, whose artistic ability was put to good use in the packaging of biscuits. In the enlarged and modernised bakery and showrooms on the A35 beyond Bridport, hundreds of visitors call each week to watch the biscuits being made and, if they desire, make their purchases.

About 50,000 sweet biscuits are made every day, and sold within a forty-mile radius of the village of Morcombelake. Dorset Ginger, Walnut Crunches and Golden Caps are made all the year round, but if you want to see the Dorset knobs being made, you will have to visit the bakery between January and March — for economic reasons they are only manufactured for three months of the year. Each biscuit is individually made by hand and, with three slow bakings, the whole process takes eight to ten hours.

The Dorset Knob factory

# LYME REGIS

The Cobb, 800 feet long, was built during the reign of Edward I as protection for the fishing fleet and as a convenience for vessels engaged in Continental trade. A curving breakwater which offers shelter on both sides, it is thought to be one of the earliest artificial harbours. It was Edward who made the town a borough in 1279, and the appellation Regis was added.

In Edward III's reign, Lyme sent four ships to the Siege of Calais in 1347, only one less than Portsmouth. Retaliation came later when the French landed, on several occasions, to sack and burn the town.

The little port played its part in Armada days and sent two ships to fight the Spaniards. During the Civil War, the brave folk of Lyme successfully held the town for Parliament in spite of an attack by 4000 Royalist soldiers. In 1685, the Duke of Monmouth landed on the beach west of the Cobb to start his ill-fated rebellion against James II. The Dorset men who rallied to his cause were cut to pieces at the Battle of Sedgemoor.

Museum open daily April-Sept 10.30-1.00; 2.30-5.00

Price guide A

Lyme Regis is famous for several reasons — as would be expected of such an ancient place. It is one of the oldest 'Loyal and Ancient Boroughs' in Britain with its known roots going back to AD 755 in the days of Kenwulf, king of the West Saxons.

It would seem that the artists who designed Lyme created a beautiful town to remind travellers crossing the western border into Devon that they were leaving a lovely county. The town is centred on that remarkable harbour construction, the Cobb, and the main roads drop and curve down the hillsides to meet at the sandy beach.

Looking out past the Cobb towards Golden Cap

Walk to the western beach beyond the Cobb and sit for a while to visualise the events which began in the early morning of June 11 1685. Overnight, three strange ships had anchored in the bay. They flew no flags and no guns were obvious. Fishermen pronounced the ships to be Dutch.

The town quickly became alive as anxious townsfolk came to see what was happening. When seven boats set out for the shore loaded with armed men, it was too much for Mayor Gregory Alford, who ordered the alarm drums to be sounded and hastened to Honiton on his horse. As the boats drew close, a tall man in a curled wig, wearing a hat with black ostrich feathers, was observed in the leading craft. His dress was purple and he wore a star on his breast. He landed, doffed his hat and, as the crews gathered around him, they all knelt in prayer. In the silence that followed, the standard bearer unfurled a green banner which bore the words 'Fear nothing but God'. The Duke of Monmouth, eldest, but illegitimate son of Charles II, had arrived to claim the throne of England.

A few weeks later, the Star of the Order of the Garter — which he so proudly wore — would be his downfall. On the run following his defeat at Sedgemoor, and dressed as a poor shepherd, he had it in his pocket when found asleep under a hedge near Cranborne Chase.

Lyme started to flourish as a seaside resort in the 18th century. The first bathing machines arrived in 1760 and it became a fashionable resort. Princess Victoria, later to become Queen, visited the town and sailed from that arm of the Cobb which today bears her name. The thatched cottages along the seafront, where wealthy Victorians spent their holidays, can still be seen.

Thatched cottages in Marine Parade

Lyme has grown up in a strange fashion. Although once an important harbour, little development took place around the Cobb itself and the busy 'church town', a few hundred yards to the east, is linked to it by the pedestrian Marine Parade.

At the foot of Church Street, the road from Bridport, is the Town Hall, Old Market and museum. The Town Hall was rebuilt in 1887. Formerly called the 'Court of Hastings', the iron-cased door that once led to the 'lock-up' is on the north front. The Old Market is beneath the Town Hall. Beside it there is an opening leading to the Gun Cliff, now a small promenade.

Bridge Street crosses the river Buddle where an old arch of the bridge, thought to be 14th or 15th century, is a feast for antiquarians. Coombe Street is very narrow and has steps leading down to the stream. Nearby are the mill and the Leper's Well.

The parish church of St Michael the Archangel, at the foot of the town, is now only about 100 feet from the sea; because of the slipping soil, it needs constant repair. Built on a steep hillside, the church floor is on three levels with the chancel being several feet higher than the porch.

Broad Street has many excellent Georgian buildings and it is worth the climb to Sidmouth Road to see the Umbrella Cottage, a small thatched building with a conical roof.

Umbrella Cottage, Sidmouth Road

Lyme tries to forget its past of battle and bloodshed and prefers to remember that 'Jane Austen lived here'. At the beginning of the 19th century she chose it as a location for her last great novel *Persuasion*. Even Tennyson came to Lyme to see the place on the Cobb where the fictitious Louisa Musgrove fell — a key point in the narrative.

The Philpot Museum has one of Britain's leading authors, John Fowles, as its honorary curator. In 1980, Lyme was transformed into a Victorian town for the filming of his best-seller *The French Lieutenant's Woman*.

Geology naturally plays a major role amongst the exhibits in the museum, for the area around Lyme is of exceptional geological interest. Casts of plants and animals dating from millions of years ago are on display, and there are showcases of seashells and fossilised remains. Ammonites and belemnites are among the numerous exhibits, and can still be found under the cliffs, but the pride of the museum is the fossilised fish-lizard (or ichthyosaurus to the learned), which is estimated to have lived an incredible 140 million years ago!

The Town Hall and Fossil Shop in Bridge Street

You can compare Roman coins with a fourpenny piece of 1844, and read an account of a trial for witchcraft. The old town's huge alarm bell, cast in 1647, hangs in the entrance hall, a reminder of the Civil War when, in 1644, the town was besieged, and you can see cannon balls and grape shot fired at that time. There are also exhibits connected with the Monmouth Rebellion which occurred some forty years later.

On show is the town fire engine of 1720, which was used for more than 150 years, and there are mementos of a visit to the town in 1895 of the American artist James Whistler.

There are also many relics from the famous Assembly Rooms and a piece of wood from its floor — on which Jane Austen danced. But the most bizarre exhibit of all is the rusty head of a boarding spike on which rebels' heads were displayed after the Battle of Sedgemoor in 1685.

# WEST DORSET

Forde Abbey.

Thorncombe.

Pilsdon
Pen.

Broadwindsor
B3162

Beaminster.

Bettiscombe.
B3164

Parnham.

Marshwood
Vale.
B3165

Pilsdon.

B3066

Bridport.

B3157
West
Bay

.............. Coast Footpath.

# THE WESTERN HILLS

The west of Dorset, with is towering hills and curving downs, has — for some unknown reason — never attained the popularity of the east, yet west of Maiden Newton and Sherborne are some of the most beautiful and peaceful areas of England. The hilltops around Cattistock and the downhill drive into the little village of Sydling St Nicholas, and the lovely valley of the Bride river, are but two of many delightful places to explore.

Planning such journeys is half the fun, but here is a route which takes you deep into the western hills and Marshwood Vale, taking in a few historically interesting villages.

As you leave Bridport travelling west on the A35, turn right about quarter of a mile past the Bridport Post Office on to the B3162. Pass through Allington and, after 1½ miles, turn left at Dottery crossroads where a house stands which was formerly the Blue Ball Inn. Now you are entering the Marshwood Vale, known to those who love this place as the Vale of the Blue Mist, because in early summer it is carpeted with bluebells. Soon you arrive at Broadoak, but avoid all turnings until you reach the Shave Cross Inn.

There has been an inn on this site for 700 years and it was used by pilgrims visiting the shrine of St Wite in nearby Whitchurch Canicorum. The inn is worth visiting and has ancient beams. Legend has it that Atte the Shaver worked here, shaving the heads of the pilgrims. As you might expect, people will tell you that his ghost is sometimes seen in the garden.

On leaving, bear right. Half a mile on, a right-hand turning will lead you to the village of Pilsdon. Tarry awhile and, after visiting the little towerless 13th-century church with quaint stone faces on opposite walls, seek out the Tudor Manor House.

Here, during the Civial War era, lived the Cavalier Sir Hugh Wyndham, a Royalist judge. When the future Charles II was fleeing

King Charles II slept here

from Worcester, it was believed that he was sheltering at Sir Hugh's house. His pursuers ransacked the house and gave the womenfolk a good going over because they thought he was disguised as a woman. It is said that Sir Hugh fumed and raged in the Hall throughout the search. Their intelligence was at fault, for while they searched, Charles was hidden at the home of Sir Hugh's nephew at Trent, and dressed as a servant.

Pilsdon Pen is the next stop — the highest point in Dorset, 909 feet above the sea. The road brings you to a car layby a short walk from the summit where, on a clear day, you can picnic against a background of breathtaking views from this ancient British hillfort. Just over two miles away in an easterly direction is Lewesdon Hill, 15 feet shorter than Pilsdon. The pair are known as the Cow and Calf by sailors — for they are visible from the sea. Both are National Trust properties. Looking south, you see the Marshwood Vale with the river Char wending its way to the sea at Charmouth, while on the lower western slopes of Pilsdon Pen is Racedown Farm, where Wordsworth first started to write seriously. The heights of Pilsdon consoled his sister Dorothy, who pined for her Lakeland hills. The view beyond encompasses Axminster and the green valley watered by the Axe, the Yarty and the Corry Brook.

Left and below: Views from Pilsdon Pen

View from Pilsdon Pen - the highest point in Dorset

Descending from the summit of Pilsdon, continue in a north-easterly direction along the B3164 to Broadwindsor — site of another chapter in the flight of Charles II from defeat at Worcester in 1651. When he arrived at Charmouth to meet the boat which was to have conveyed him to France, the captain did not turn up — his wife was suspicious of 'odd goings on' and would not let him out. So Charles had to hasten back to his hide-out at Trent, the home of Colonel Wyndham, nephew of Sir Hugh of Pilsdon.

Meanwhile, he needed somewhere to sleep, and on a plaque affixed to an ancient house in Broadwindsor village, we read that 'Charles II slept here on September 23 1651'. It does not tell you that this was probably part of a larger building called the Castle Inn and that Charles, disguised as a servant to Lord Wilmot, and a Miss Coningsly, were trapped upstairs when boisterous officers of a company of Parliamentary troops, searching for Charles, took over the bar below. Luckily, the birth of a child to one of the camp followers caused such an uproar in the village that the officers left to sort it out, and Charles and his party hastened away.

Return to the car and follow the B3162 road to Drimpton, a sleepy hamlet with a small inn. Continue to Hornash crossroads. If you have an Ordnance Survey map, sheet 193, the reference is 398046. Continue south to Birdsmoorgate (392009). Descend from the ridge, taking the B3164 for about half a mile, and bear right for Bettiscombe. Here you will find the church of St Stephen — a smugglers' haunt in the 19th century — and the Manor House, the home of the Pinney family. A macabre legend is attached to the Manor concerning a human skull which was once housed in the building. The skull was supposed to be that of a devoted negro servant. Whenever it was moved from its resting place a scream was heard, and ill fortune was sure to follow.

After passing Marshwood Manor, cross over the first crossroads to a T-junction. Turn right and a minor road will lead you to Vale House Farm where you turn left for Whitchurch Canonicorum. The fine church of St Candida is known as the Cathedral of the Marshwood Vale. This lovely parish takes its name from St Wite, also known as Candida, a Breton princess. In the 5th century she went to live in Brittany with her second husband, Fragan. The legend of Wite tells how she was carried off by pirates, but escaped when her virtue was assailed. Then, with her left hand chopped off, she walked back on the water to Brittany, where she died. She was canonised and, in AD 919, her remains were brought to Whitchurch by Breton immigrants. Within the church you will find her shrine.

The tour nears its end and the road leads uphill past the Five Bells where you can enjoy the views from Ryall before descending to Chideock and Seatown where the coast is blessed with myriads of fossils. But that will have to wait for another day's exploring. Bridport, the starting point of this Marshwood Vale tour, is only three miles away along the A35.

Pilsdon Manor

# FORDE ABBEY

Open Sun, Wed, bank
holidays May-Sept
2.00-6.00
Gardens only in April and
Oct, Sun 2.00-4.30

Price guide C

Dorset won the lovely Forde Abbey from Devon in a boundary change in 1842 and, with it, the parish of Thorncombe. One well-known historian has described it as 'the object of greatest importance on the west frontier of Dorset'.

The magnificent old abbey has its roots in the early 12th century. Monks who had been at a monastery founded by Sir Richard Brioniis in Devon were offered a site by his sister who lived at Thorncombe. As it was near a ford over the river Axe, it became known as Forde Abbey. The monks built on high ground by a spring which flowed into the river, and it worked their mechanical appliances which included a corn mill and saw-mill.

Many Devonshire families, among them the Courtenays and de Pomeroys, swelled the monks' funds from time to time. With the exception of the church and the infirmary, most of the original buildings remain intact, including the chapter house, which is now a private chapel, dormitory and a 12th-century refectory. It is a great joy to visit this ancient place because unlike so many abbeys of this period, it is no ruin silhouetted against the skyline, but still lives after 800 years.

Baldwin, a man of humble birth, was Forde's most colourful Abbot. He became Bishop of Worcester and succeeded Thomas a Becket as Archbishop of Canterbury. He died while accompanying King Richard I on a Crusade to the Holy Land.

The last Abbot, Thomas Chard, who died in in 1544, did much to beautify Forde and his reconstructed cloister and refectory remain as he left them.

Four hundred years ago, Forde Abbey became a private home and families with illustrious names have lived there. At the Dissolution of the Monasteries in the 16th century the abbey was granted to Richard Pollard. He was followed by the Pouletts and the Roswells. During the Civil War it was occupied by Sir Edmund Prideaux, Attorney General to the Commonwealth, and its ancient walls were spared from destruction. Prideaux employed the famous Inigo Jones to make alterations to the building.

Sir Francis Gwyn inherited by marriage in 1702. He was Secretary of War to Queen Anne who, for services rendered, presented him with the celebrated copies of the Raphael tapestry cartoons. The originals were made by Brussels weavers brought over by Charles I to instruct British workers. Several copies were made but the Forde set, now in the saloon, are considered to be very fine. The scenes shown include the Saviour's charge to St Peter, the miraculous draught of fishes, the Saints Peter and John healing the lame man, and Ananias and Sapphira.

The present owners open the house and gardens for limited periods. The 15 acres of gardens are very beautiful, with shady trees and ponds and water gardens. There are a great variety of flowering shrubs.

# PARNHAM
## BEAMINSTER

Parnham tells the story of successive generations who have lived in its enchanting valley among the deeply-folded hills of West Dorset for over four hundred years. Once a manor, the heart of a large estate, the house grew in size and grandeur and now reflects the splendour of its history. Its mellowed walls, framed by buttresses rising to pinnacles against the sky, were embattled by Royal assent.

The gardens echo the building's distinctive features; balustraded terraces, sweeping lawns, topiary and cascading water contrast with the shaded riverbank, the magnificent trees of the woodland and the more intimate planting of the courtyards and borders.

Stained glass, carved wood and early Romayne plasterwork decorate the interior, which has been lovingly restored in sympathy with its age and architecture; the contents, though, demonstrate Parnham's dedication to fine individual craftsmanship and design of the twentieth century as the home of John Makepeace, the designer, and his famous furniture-making workshops. There is a shop selling some of the smaller items of fine craftsmanship made at Parnham. Exhibitions by contemporary artists, designers and craftsmen are held each month.

The house, gardens, exhibitions and workshops are open regularly each year from April to October; please write or telephone for details.

*The School for Craftsmen in Wood at Parnham is not open to visitors.*

Parnham House, Beaminster, Dorset, DT8 3NA. Telephone Beaminster (0308) 862204

# PARNHAM HOUSE

Open Sun, Wed, bank
holidays April-Oct
10.00-5.00

Price guide C

Dorset should be proud of Parnham, a beautiful golden Ham stone house in a wooded vale known as the valley of the pear trees, among the unspoilt hills of west Dorset. A house was there in medieval days, but it was completely rebuilt in the time of Elizabeth I by Sir Robert Strode. Successive generations added to the house using the same distinctive stone from quarries at Ham Hill in Somerset.

The Strodes were staunch Royalists and sheltered King Charles II during his flight through the West Country in 1651. The Great Hall was the scene of a brutal murder when Lady Anne Strode was beheaded by the sword of a Cromwellian soldier.

The Strode rule ended when, in 1776, the estate passed to Sir William Oglander of the Isle of Wight. His grandson commissioned John Nash to enlarge and embellish the house in 1810, and castellations, buttesses and pinnacles were added.

A new chapter in the history of Parnham was written in 1896. Vincent Robinson bought it for £22,000 and lived there surrounded by pets and his collection of Renaissance furniture and European works of art. Following his death in 1909, the contents of the house were sold.

Before the Great War, Hans Sauer reinstated the Tudor interiors previously altered by Nash and installed some of the services still in use today. Dr Sauer was responsible for the bold landscaping of the grounds, the building of terraces, water channels, balustrades, rotundas and the front court.

Parnham was bought by the Rhodes-Moorhouse family in 1912 at the persuasion of their newly-married son William, an intrepid pilot who had flown across the channel in record time accompanied by his wife and a reporter. His courage was demonstrated for the last time during the Great War, when he flew from France to bomb Bruges Station, at that time in German hands. Having delivered his load, carried in the passenger seat, he was wounded while still over enemy lines and died after landing his plane safely back in France. William Rhodes-Moorhouse was the first airman to be awarded the Victoria Cross.

Some 26 years later his son was killed in the Battle of Britain. Both these men and other members of the family are buried in a private graveyard on the hill to the west of Parnham, on the spot chosen by William and his wife for a cottage in anticipation of his return from the war.

Parnham became a Country Club for a while in the 1920s. The Bullivant family then took up residence and lived there in a grand manner throughout the 1930s until the house was requisitioned at the start of the Second World War. At first it was used as an army hospital and later as the HQ for the 16th Infantry Division of the American Army. Eventually it became a prisoner-of-war camp, and in due course a private nursing home.

Then in 1976 Parnham was aquired by John Makepeace, one of the world's best designers and makers of fine furniture. He immediately began a programme of restoration, and the conversion of parts of the building into furniture-making workshops.

educational charity, the school took its first students in 1977. Now 20 young people, of both sexes and including several from overseas, are given an intensive two-year course of instruction in the many techniques of practical craftsmanship in wood, the principles of design, business management and marketing — in short, all the skills they need to set up and run their own businesses as self-employed designer-craftsmen. The school is residential; what was the servants' wing now contains the refectory, kitchens, study-bedrooms and drawing offices and the students are looked after by an able housekeeper and her assistants.

The great hall of Parnham looks very much as it must have looked in Tudor times, with its enormous oak ceiling beams and purlins, its tall windows with the blazons of the Strode family in stained glass, its minstrels' gallery and screen, its massive fireplace and its honey-coloured stone walls. But no antique tapestries or Old Masters hang on the walls; no Jacobean coffers or Sheraton escritoires are to be seen. Instead, recently completed pieces from the furniture workshops are on show.

The drawing room was restored in 1978; the intricate and delicately-coloured plasterwork of its ceiling sets off the pale shades of its oak panelling and the exuberant swags and cornucopia carved in limewood on the mantel. A huge south-facing ceiling-height bay window lights the exhibitions which are one of Parnham's principal attractions for visitors.

Surrounded by parkland and great trees, Parnham's tranquil exterior belies the dynamism of the activities within. John Makepeace designs unique pieces of furniture for customers with a variety of needs — private householders, collectors, eminent societies, universities, the Church and great corporations. A team of skilled young craftsmen transforms these ideas, under his direction, into objects which exhibit the quality of design and craftsmanship upon which his reputation is based. Predominantly indigenous timbers such as oak, elm, ash, cherry, holly and laburnum are used, but also some exotic woods such as Andaman padouk, Indian rosewood and paldao from the Phillipines. All these are naturally seasoned at Parnham. Leather, ivory, stainless steel, silk, silver leaf and gold leaf are also used.

One wing of the house — formerly dilapidated lofts and stabling — contains the workshops of The School for Craftsmen in Wood. Under the aegis of the Parnham Trust, a non-profit-making

In the library is a personal collection of work, both primitive and highly technological, by other craftsmen whom John Makepeace has come to know in his foreign travels - it includes an Australian aboriginal bark container and a plaque engraved by laser, for example. There are craftsmen's tools and a display of some of the thousands of different timbers found around the world.

Parnham does have a four-poster bed — but Queen Elizabeth never slept in it! It was made in the Makepeace workshops in 1976 from the wood of a single English yew and the sensuous curves of its posts reflect the natural curve which was in the tree when it was felled.

# BEAMINSTER

West Dorset has changed much less than most of southern England in the last 150 years. Beaminster's encircling hills — for it is set in a bowl of oolitic limestone uplands — are still green and woody, and give birth to the river Brit which has cut itself an exit southwards through them, on its way to Bridport.

When you approach Beaminster — except from the south — you see it first from above, and very pleasant it is to look upon. It is a place of mellow stone, honey-coloured buildings, most of which date from the late 17th or 18th centuries.

The small town nestles in countryside considered by many to be amongst the most beautiful and varied in England. Once it was the forgotten part of the county, but now more and more visitors are coming to know the area which is ideal walker's country.

The church is in Somerset style and, as you approach from the hills, the tall tower stands high with the town houses grouped around it, like a shepherd standing in the centre of a flock of sheep. It can have changed little since the Dorset poet William Barnes, descending from the hills wrote

> Sweet Be'mi'ster, that bist abound
> By green an' woody hills all round
> wi' hedges, reachen up between
> A thousan' vields of zummer green.

Monument to George and Catherine Strode of Parnham in the church

Ancient burial grounds and encampments on the surrounding hills testify to the presence of man in this vicinity since prehistoric times. Beaminster is recorded as Bebingmynster in the year 872. According to historian Richard Hine, the most likely derivation of the name is from the two Old English words *beam* — a tree, and *mynster* — a church, hence the church of trees or amidst trees. The manor was a possession of the see of Sarum at the time of the Domesday Survey of 1086.

Unfortunately, fire devastated Beaminster three times in two centuries. In 1644, during the Civil War, a particularly destructive blaze occurred when the Royalist army of Prince Maurice lay in the town. According to a contemporary account, it began with the discharge of a musket in the gable of a house in North Street by a Hungarian trooper. Further fires in 1684 and 1781 also did a lot of damage.

The small town of Beaminster still remembers when its Gardens and Allotments Society featured on television when they won a gold medal at the Chelsea Flower Show. In fact, it is such a busy place that it boasts 55 different clubs, societies and youth organisations.

Two miles south-east of Beaminster is Mapperton, with its old Manor House. The magnificent gardens are open to the public. Nearby is Netherbury; the little river Brit flows through the valley of this cider-making village, one of the most beautiful in Dorset.

The church

The Square

The Square dominates this neat little town, with a market cross erected in 1906 on the site of a medieval version. It is built of local Ham stone, with niched pinnacles of Portland stone. Among the quaint streets which radiate from the Square you will find a Fleet Street, but there is no bustle of newspaper presses here. It has a public hall erected to commemorate the coronation of Edward VII.

# NORTH DORSET

Worldwide Butterflies

Yeovil.
Sherborne.
Castle
Sturminster
Newton
Shaftesbury.
East Stour
Blandford
Forum

BLACKMOOR VALE

# WORLDWIDE BUTTERFLIES

Open daily April-Oct;
10.00-5.00
Price guide C

As the explorer nears the Somerset border at Yeovil, he will discover a unique farm in the grounds of Compton House at Over Compton. Worldwide Butterflies and the Lullingstone Silk Farm have no parallel elsewhere in Britain or overseas.

In the setting of the house and its grounds, visitors see butterflies alive and flying in exotic jungle surroundings. In favourable conditions, temperate species can be seen outside in the breeding grounds, together with their caterpillars. Chrysalids and cocoons are laid out, and butterflies hatch out daily, sometimes right in front of your eys. The collections of butterflies are extremely varied, educational, informative and a riot of colour. The Lullingstone Silk Farm demonstrates the rearing of silkworms, and the process of reeling the silk from the cocoons.

Worldwide's story will delight anyone with a spirit of adventure. It all started when a young saucepan salesman at Harrods, Robert Gooden, started rearing butterflies in his spare time. As the work grew, he moved to Charmouth and, encouraged by his parents, took over an attic, and later a small building in the paddock.

Silkworms feeding on mulberry leaves

In 1962 Robert Gooden made a tour of the Far East to establish contacts and gain experience of butterflies in the tropics. Soon a butterfly exhibition was opened in Charmouth, followed by another in Lyme Regis. A turning point came in 1966 when the Charmouth premises were outgrown, and it was decided to move to the grounds of the family home, Compton House, near Sherborne. In the same year, a new showroom was opened at Brighton.

Purple emperor

So many visitors crowded in, that far better provision had to be made for them. In 1976 new breeding areas were opened and the experimental new jungle built, but in April the sad news came that Compton House was to be auctioned out of the family. Then Robert and his wife, Rosemary, decided on a gamble which might enable them to buy the great house. They sold the Brighton showroom and even their magnificent Heidelberg printing press, on which they produced their high quality colour brochures, to raise cash.

It was make or break for Worldwide Butterflies because it was not only a case of purchasing the decaying house, but also of restoring it — not only to become their home, but the home of the butterflies as well. The proud opening was in 1978.

At about that time, the Gooddens acquired the ailing, famous Lullingstone Silk Farm which had been started in the early thirties by Zoe, Lady Hart Dyke, at Lullingstone Castle in Kent, and which had moved to Hertfordshire in 1957. On her death in 1975, it was decided to close the farm which had provided silk for robes for the Coronation of King George VI and Queen Elizabeth, for the dress worn by Princess Elizabeth at her wedding, the Coronation Robes in 1953, and the robes for the Investiture of the Prince of Wales.

The Gooddens added Lullingstone Silk Farm to the Worldwide empire and continued the royal tradition by making silk for Princess Diana's wedding dress in 1981.

The biggest attraction of the new display areas is undoubtedly the Butterfly House. The original butterfly house has been replaced with one which gives more shelter from adverse weather conditions, but still allows the extra ventilation required by temperate species. This new house is filled with rare visitors to Britain such as the Camberwell beauty and the large tortoiseshell. Throughout the season there are also the commoner butterflies, such as peacocks, small tortoiseshells, commas and brimstones which prefer the conditions of the Butterfly House to the lush tropical surroundings of the Palm House or the Jungle. But tropical butterflies are living there too — passionflower butterflies flitting about in search of just the right place to lay their eggs. Australian lacewings have established themselves and have bred for the first time at Compton House. Swallowtails from India and Japan are laying eggs on the foodplants and producing myriads of exotic caterpillars to carry

Compton House

on the next generation of butterflies. These are used not only for display purposes, but are sent to amateur enthusiasts, schools and colleges and research establishments all over the world.

Adult butterflies live for only a matter of days on average, though exceptional species can live for months. Robert and Rosemary Goodden have found that in the conditions of the new Butterfly House some species are surviving longer. One female Japanese swallowtail is so old that only a part of her wings is left, yet she still flies about happily laying eggs, while the next generation — her children — are on the wing laying their eggs around her. Robert Goodden says he has plans for additional butterfly houses in the future with conditions suiting butterflies that have hitherto been tricky to breed.

The gardens of Compton House are open to the public, incorporating the very colourful Butterfly Gardens which, on sunny days in mid to late summer, can attract scores of wild butterflies. Areas of wild habitat are carefully preserved on the Compton Estate to encourage butterflies to breed in the locality.

Via the gardens, visitors can see the newly opened rooms in the south wing of the house where there is a special habitat display, using some of the exhibits which came from the National Butterfly Museum recently auctioned at Sothebys. Robert Goodden managed to buy a fine set of six display cases devoted to British butterflies arranged according to their habitat requirements. Other displays, which include specimens arranged in natural settings, show butterflies of a South Pacific island and a scene at a Malaysian stream.

*Papilio bianor,* from Japan

Perhaps you are wondering how a Harrods salesman was connected with this stately home. There has been a Manor of Over Compton since before the Domesday Book (1086). During the Civil War the Abingdons held Compton and it saw much action. In 1645 Fairfax led the victorious Parliamentary army through the Comptons.

In 1736, George Abingdon sold his inheritance to Robert Goodden who died in 1764. In 1766 the second son — another Robert — inherited and at 28 was made High Sheriff of Dorset. During his life he made substantial alterations and additions to the church, and it is his statue in the family pew today. He was also responsible for laying out the parkland with its many old lime trees, horse chestnuts and Spanish chestnuts, planes and tulip tree. His brother Wyndham succeeded him, and his son John took over in 1839 and was responsible for rebuilding the front of the house in the Tudor style of Montacute House — probably to please his bride, Anne Phelips of Montacute. The stained glass window of the main staircase bears the arms of Goodden and Phelips. Col. J.R.P. Goodden, next in line, added the south wing and also became a High Sheriff. For over 100 years the church living was held by just two of the family, the Rev. Wyndham Goodden (60 years) and Canon Edward Goodden who died in 1924.

The end of the great Compton era started with the First World War and, in the 1920s, much of the land was sold off. The Second World War was the final death blow. The family moved out to make way for Westlands drawing office in 1941. During the years since the war the house fell into decay, and when, in 1976, the eldest Goodden son, John, put it up for auction, Compton was saved by the butterflies.

Under Worldwide Butterflies, Compton House has been restored, and now Robert and Rosemary Goodden have acquired the rest of the original gardens, shrubbery and some adjoining land. The gardens, in less than 10 years, have been restored from pastureland and already have an established air. The land is being laid out as a natural habitat to demonstrate to visitors how wild areas can be created to encourage future generations of butterflies.

# SHERBORNE

Museum open Tue-Sat
April-Oct 10.30-12.30,
3.00-4.30; Sun 3.00-5.00
Nov-Mar Tue and Sat only
Price guide A

As you come down from the hills and enter Sherborne, you are quickly aware that this is one of England's most attractive towns and that the people care for it and keep its ancient properties neat and tidy.

It may be as well for explorers to book in at one of the town's excellent inns because you will be reluctant to leave its medieval buildings, great abbey, church, almshouses and two castles. It is one of Dorset's showpieces in a green valley.

The Saxons called it Scirburne, the place of the clear stream. They built the mother cathedral of all south-west England there, and its first bishop was St Aldhelm. It remained a cathedral until 1075, the year the see moved to Old Sarum. Two kings of Wessex were buried there.

At the Dissolution of the Monasteries in 1539, the townsfolk purchased the building and made it their parish church. So Sherborne Abbey, founded in 705 and famous for its glorious fan-vaulting, became part of our national heritage. The great building has been restored over the centuries but some of the original Saxon work can be seen at the west end of the church. In 1925, Sherborne was made a suffragen see and its bishop is the area bishop for Dorset.

The museum and abbey gateway

The warm yellow stone tower of the abbey dominates many other historical buildings. Beneath it are the almshouses founded in 1437 and known as St John the Baptist and St John the Evangelist. They house 20 elderly men and women. The building was enlarged in 1858 and 1866.

Sherborne School courtyard, and the abbey

Also near the abbey is the Conduit. Formerly an ablution area for monks, it was moved to its present site on the Parade from the cloisters, and is now without windows or doors.

Sherborne School was endowed as a grammar school by Edward VI in 1550, although there had been a school there since 705 when St Aldhelm was bishop. 700 boys now attend this famous public school situated north of the abbey, with some of the former monastic buildings incorporated into the modern additions.

An historian writing about the school gives food for thought. 'It is the most venerable of all institutions in this ancient place, with a life of almost 12 centuries; older than the English realm itself, and but two centuries younger than the first West Saxon settlement in Britain. That is a long history, but it is all written on these buildings for him that has eyes to see'.

The charming houses in the narrow streets were built during several centuries. Of particular interest is the Julian on the Green in Cheap Street, and the restored West Mill on the south-west outskirts of the town. The mill, on the banks of the river Yeo, has medieval foundations and was restored in the 1970s, when boys from Sherborne School initiated an interest in the then derelict building. The work continues with the help of the boys.

The museum of this very old town adjoins the ancient and picturesque abbey gateway. A record of 13 centuries of the town's known history is contained in what was a 19th-century house. Sherborne's oldest features are the castle and the abbey. Both of these are fully illustrated and their histories documented. There is a six by five foot model of the hill-top castle, which was built early in the 12th century. Exhibits connected with the abbey include a display of full-sized colour reproductions from the Sherborne Missal, a book dated to about 1400 containing the service of Mass for the Christian year, richly decorated with scrolls, birds and flowers in bright colours.

In the 1950s, a Victorian doll's house was bought at a local sale and, after a good deal of refurbishing and decorating, its three storeys were furnished in the Victorian style. The house is believed to date from around 1870, and the resident dolls have even earlier origins.

There is much more of local interest — prints and photos of buildings and personalities, wildlife, geological specimens, a collection of flower paintings, country bygones and pottery.

*Capability Brown's gift
for landscaping, gives visitors to
Sherborne a lot of pleasure*

**Brown's** *gift shop, The Parade,
Sherborne, has the same capability.*

# SHERBORNE CASTLE

Open Easter Saturday-end of Sept; Thur, Sat, Sun and Bank Holiday Mon only; 2.00-6.00
Price guide D (castle and grounds)
C (grounds only)

Sherborne's castles are situated about a mile east of the town centre — the old ruin separated from the new castle by a magnificent lake.

The old castle, situated on a rocky knoll at Castleton, is scheduled as an ancient monument. Bishop Roger (1107-1139) erected this castle, and the gatehouse, portions of the curtain wall, the chapel, the keep and the domestic buildings still remain. The construction work is considered to have been much in advance of its time, and it would appear to be one of the earliest castles of the concentric type. Excavations over the years have revealed that originally the castle covered a larger area than the present ruin. Traces of an elaborate entrance have been found outside the north curtain wall and the foundations of towers on the wall have been discovered. A well has been found and cleared to a depth of 50 feet, and a large kitchen traced by its foundations.

The enclosed site is about 3½ acres in extent with each corner cut off the rectangular layout giving an eight-faced curtain wall, formerly 26 feet in height and seven feet thick. It was surrounded by a dry rock-cut moat 30 feet in depth. The keep was approximately 70 feet high, and a fine Norman window still exists on the north side of the chapel. The gatehouse, three-storeyed, is mainly Norman with some Tudor windows.

The castle was seized by King Stephen when Bishop Roger was disgraced, and held by the Crown for many years. In 1599 Queen Elizabeth gave the castle to Sir Walter Raleigh, who had fallen in love with the town, but he forfeited it to ,King James when he, too was disgraced.

The old castle was besieged twice during the Civil War in 1642 and again in 1645, when Cromwell himself watched General Fairfax blow it up. The present Castleton church was built from some of the rubble.

Raleigh built the present castle as a hunting lodge in 1594. He described it as his 'fortunes fold', and visitors to the site will understand why. Set in a natural amphitheatre of wooded hills, Capability Brown's 18th-century landscaping can only have enhanced the beautiful natural setting known to Raleigh and his family.

The exterior of the castle, with its forest of chimneys and mysterious heraldic beasts guarding the balustrades and turrets, provokes many comments and ideas. Possibly the greatest surprise to most visitors is the stucco rendering. This is not a 20th-century device to cover the wear and tear of four centuries' weathering, but a repaired version of that used by Sir Walter Raleigh in 1594. Thus the castle is probably one of the earliest buildings in the country to be treated in this way.

The atmosphere and modest size of the castle rooms reflect a happy family home where comfort seems more important than grandeur. Even the most imposing room — with the Raleigh Coat of Arms on the ceiling — has three beautifully decorated fireplaces, the warmth from which would have been greatly appreciated by his guests in winter.

The Digby family, when they were granted the Sherborne Estates in 1617, were considered an ancient and distinguished family and are still owners of the castle. As a result of this continuity of ownership, the building reflects every period of nearly 400 years of history. For instance, the contrast between the Strawberry Hill Gothic Library and the Jacobean panelled Oakroom brings alive the character of the differing centuries with startling clarity. Among the marvellous furniture, paintings and porcelain you will see as a visitor, are the world-famous painting of Elizabeth I in procession, the rare Digby Tilting Helm and the exquisite collection of oriental porcelain made by the present owner's brother.

The Digby wings, added to Raleigh's original rectangular building, created an unusual frontage reflected in the river Yeo, which widens into a lake between the new and the old castles.

The old castle and the new

# WILLIAM BARNES OF DORSET

William Barnes and Thomas Hardy had little in common; Dorset was inspiration to both, but Barnes chose to record only the gentle and beautiful aspects of the county, whereas Hardy used its dramatic landscapes as settings for human tragedy. Both writers died within a mile of each other and have graves on the outskirts of the county town.

The love story of Barnes, the romantic who started his life in the lovely Vale of Blackmoor and later came to Dorchester, where he met the love of his life, Julia, rivals the story of Robert Browning and Elizabeth Barrett. The explorer will find most of the places mentioned have changed little since the 19th century when William Barnes strolled along the banks of the twisting, sleepy Stour composing poetry.

He was born into a 'downstart' family at Rushay on Bagber Heath, but the little farm has long since vanished although some local farmers can show you the site. Close by on the A357 is Lydlinch with its inspirational church bells. ('For Lydlinch Bells be good for sound, and liked by all the neighbours round').

The mill at Hinton St Mary, where young William Barnes came to play and so discovered the Stour, can be reached via the B3092 out of Sturminster Newton. Turn left down a lane at the far end of the village of Hinton. At the end is the cloty Stour, so named because of the yellow clote lily which grows in profusion on this Dorset river, and the derelict mill which featured as a French mill in the television film serial *Fair Stood the Wind for France*.

The river twists a couple of miles downstream to Sturminster Newton, as lovely a minster town as any in England. The centre is a planners' nightmare with houses and shops of all shapes and sizes crowded onto narrow thoroughfares.

Any resident will be pleased to show you where William Barnes went to school, and you can sit on the steps of the ancient cross in the Market Square as he did 180 years ago. There are excellent inns in which the explorer can refresh himself before returning to the river via the old bridge which threatens you with deportation if you damage it. The river drifts past Fiddleford Mill where, as a boy, Barnes toiled in the fields.

The Blackmoor Vale, of which Sturminster was once the capital, stretches from the source of the Stour just over the Dorset boundary, south of the Shaftesbury Heights to the eastern hills of Hod and Hambledon, and these places feature in his writings. If the explorer is interested in the life of this Dorset author, he must journey to Dorchester as the young Barnes did in 1818, with a farewell poem to the girls of the vale which ended:

> Tis in vain! her whose beauty can alien my love
> From Eliza I shall never find;
> And naught but the sheen from her
>     eyes can remove,
> The gloom that envelopes my mind.

Market Square, Sturminster Newton

How wrong he was we shall see. He became an engrossing clerk to a firm of solicitors. One day, standing across the road from the Kings Arms in the High Street, he watched a beautiful girl step down from the stage-coach and vowed to marry her. Julia had come into his life, and the girls of the Blackmoor Vale were forgotten.

He was in love, but it was to be a troubled affair. He courted Julia on the banks of the river Frome, which runs parallel with the A352 on the right as you enter Dorchester. Walk along the banks as this young couple did and pass the Hangman's Cottage, still there in the shadow of the prison.

Julia's father, a supervisor of excise, thought William a layabout. To impress him, William became a schoolmaster and, in 1823, went to Mere — just over Dorset's northern boundary — and eventually took over the Chantry House School. In the lovely garden there he composed some of his beautiful sonnets. The arbour where he wrote is still there, but the Chantry is a private residence. He married Julia in 1827 and brought her to Mere. 'On a happy day — happy as the first of a most happy wedded life — I brought into it Julia Miles, bespoken by an early choice, than which I cannot conceive a better.' He was at the peak of his happiness and, on leaving in 1835, penned these lines:

> No more, at breezy eve, or dewy morn,
> My gliding scythe shall sheer thy mossy green;
> My busy hands shall never more adorn.
> My eyes no more may see, this peaceful scene.
> But still sweet spot, wherever I may be,
> My love-led soul will wander back to thee.

The Stour at Fiddleford Mill

He opened a school at Dorchester in South Street, and Julia bore six children. In 1852, however, she died. William was inconsolable and, until the end of his life, daily wrote her name in his diary.

At 47 years of age, he took Holy Orders and preached his first sermon as curate, at Whitcombe. You will find Whitcombe on the Dorchester — Broadmayne road, A352, four miles out of Dorchester. The little church, shrouded by trees, is on a downhill bend and has been kept as a memorial to Barnes. The pulpit is as he left it after his last service there, given when he was 86. It was to be his last sermon before he died.

Barnes was buried from his last home, the Rectory at Winterborne Came. This house of overhanging thatch can be seen between Whitcombe and Dorchester, on the same side of the road as Whitcombe church.

There, as he was dying, he penned the touching poem which ended thus:

And oft do come a saddened hour,
When there must goo away,
One well beloved to our hearts core,
Vor long, perhaps for aye,
And Oh! It is a touchen thing
The loving heart must rue
To hear behind his last farewell
The geate a-vallen to.

The final line refers to the gate falling shut.

Whitcombe Church

On his last evening he was praying with his daughter, Laura, and at the end of the prayer 'Lighten Our Darkness' he mumbled a long poem but only these words were remembered.

Dry our eyes in weeping.
Shut our eyes in sleeping.

Whitcombe Church

You can visit his grave in the corner of the churchyard at Winterborne Came. The explorer should arm himself with a copy of his *Poems of Rural Life*. This will add many more explorable locations such as Bishops Caundle, Shroton, Beaminster and the lost village of Farringdon, within a few hundred yards of his grave. All that is left is a chancel in a field. Beneath it, the poet often sat to write.

I seem to see the church's wall
And some grey tomb beneath a yew,
And hear the churchyard wicket fall
Behind the people passing through.
I seem to hear above my head
The bell that in the tower was hung;
But whither went its iron tongue
That here bemoaned the long lost dead?

If the explorer crosses a little stream he can sit beneath this ruin, unchanged in hundreds of years, and like the poet experience the peace and birdsong in a field that was Farringdon.

Cottages at Sturminster Newton

# SHAFTESBURY

Abbey Ruins Museum
open: daily, Good Fri - end
Sept; 10.00-6.30
Price guide A
Shaftesbury Local History
Museum open: Easter -
end Sept; weekdays 11.00-
5.00, Sundays 2.30-5.00
Price guide A

This quaint place atop a North Dorset hill is as pretty a town as you will see anywhere in England. Its historic fame reached a peak centuries ago and the cunning system by which the traffic bypasses the town leaves the streets peaceful. The town is too old to catch up with the bustle of the 20th century.

February day the funeral procession which crept up the hillside included the Earl of Mercia, the Bishop of Sherborne, the Abbess of Wilton and all her nuns, and many noblemen with their retinues. The king's tomb became a shrine and it is claimed that miraculous cures were carried out there.

St Peters, a Perpendicular church, and the early 19th-century town hall stand together at the top of Gold Hill. The hill has been made famous by the little Hovis boy who pushes his bicycle up the steep cobbled street for a television advertisement. Looking down from the top, a row of modest cottages on the left, and the great buttressed wall retaining the old abbey precinct on the right, form a frame for the expanse of Blackmoor Vale spread out below.

The Vale of Blackmoor from the abbey ruins

Gold Hill

Shaftesbury once boasted a castle, three mints a magnificent abbey, 12 churches and even hospitals on its 700-foot heights. All have long gone. The four market crosses — St Mary's at Gold Hill, the Fish Cross and the Butter and Cheese Crosses disappeared in the 18th century.

Shaftesbury was the site of a burgh created by King Alfred, and the abbey was founded toward the end of the 9th century for his daughter, Aethelgive, to become its first abbess. Athelstan, King Alfred's grandson, authorised the Royal Mints which struck silver coins bearing the town's name until 1272.

The town's most famous hour came on the 20th February 979 when King Edward the Martyr, murdered at Corfe Castle, dragged by his horse to Wareham and buried there, was re-interred at Shaftesbury Abbey. On that

At the top of Gold Hill is an old building once described as having been a doss-house attached to the Sun and Moon Inn, to accommodate travelling-men from the fairs and markets. Nowadays it is a museum of varied interest, but it concentrates on the several faces of Victoriana. Its two floors are closely packed with parasols, fans, dolls, needlework, elaborate valentine cards, and a lock of the great queen's hair. There is a tapestry bell-pull, with a set of the jangling bells which sent overworked house-maids scurrying, and a collection of household equipment which will take granny back to her childhood days. There is a most interesting display of old cinematograph machines and magic lanterns, with one whose flickering light was provided by a four-wick oil burner!

The Dorset button industry provided cottagers with employment when times were hard, and an assortment is shown here, starting from the original covered horn rings. You can see a quaint old 'fire-engine' of 1744, with solid wooden wheels and leather hose and buckets. Upstairs among local excavations of flint and pot, are documents and commemorative china, and there is a collection of old farming tools.

The abbey precinct wall on Gold Hill

St Peter's Church, and the museum

Inside the museum: domestic bygones, and the fire engine of 1744

You can walk in the garden and enjoy a magnificent view, and see — rather casually displayed — a stone Roman coffin decoratively used as a rock garden!

Come back to the High Street and on the L-shaped turning King Alfred's Kitchen will take your eye, because it is the only timber-framed building surviving in the town. A few steps and the explorer is walking on the main promenade of the abbey ruins, Park Walk, scheduled as an ancient monument. There are welcome seats from which to enjoy the view of the Vale of Blackmoor. Here, through a hole in the wall, is the abbey site and its own museum.

The abbey was enlarged by the Normans and became one of the richest in the land, before being destroyed during the Dissolution of the Monasteries by the Tudors.

The ruins have been excavated and the site is tastefully arranged so that the visitor can easily trace out the abbey's original design and its most important features. A small museum in the grounds contains a vast quantity of stone relics — carvings, floor tiles, pillars, bosses and capitals, together with a scale model of the complete abbey and a most interesting 'tree of Wessex' showing an unbroken royal line from Ine in 688 to the present day, ending with the marriage of Princess Anne.

Near the Grosvenor Hotel is Bimport, and the church of Holy Trinity (1841), an early work of Sir George Gilbert Scott which faces a modern cinema in the style of the 1930s. From the churchyard, a medieval wall is visible with an ogee-headed lancet, incorporated into the National School of 1847. Here also is the Abbey House, mostly Georgian. On the right of Bimport lies Castle Hill, where there is an earthwork, but not the 'castle' one might imagine.

Journey downhill to the valley and St James, a lower-level suburb, with the mullion-windowed St Edward's Chantry and the picturesque old Pump Court, with its pump standing in an open-ended quadrangle.

An interesting relic is the Byzant, to be seen in the town hall. In medieval times Shaftesbury, on a hill, had no water supply, so a bargain was made with the Lord of the Manor of Gillingham, enabling townspeople to use the springs on Enmore Green. To retain this right, the mayor, burgesses and townspeople had to go to Enmore Green carrying the Byzant (Prize Besom) which was decked with feathers, ribbons and jewels. They were received by the Lord of the Manor and dancing took place followed by a presentation to him of a pair of gloves, two wheaten loaves, a calf's head and a gallon of ale. The rest of the day was spent in feasting and dancing. This colourful ceremony has been re-enacted by the townspeople on and off for a number of years.

In the Grosvenor Hotel the famous Chevy Chase sideboard can be seen. It is carved from a solid piece of oak and has six compartments of intricate carving showing men and animals at the battle of Chevy Chase in 1388.

The explorer will be told countless stories about old Shaftesbury but this is one of the most amusing.

In 1285 the Archbishop of Canterbury excommunicated Sir Osbert Gifford for stealing two nuns at Wilton. He was absolved under the following conditions: That he should never again enter a nunnery or come into the company of nuns. That for three Sundays he should be stripped and whipped publicly at Shaftesbury and Wilton. That he should fast a number of months, and not wear a shirt for three years, but wear only rough clothes. He was to return the nuns to their nunnery for similar punishment. It is a story which appealed to Dorset historian Treves. He wrote: 'It would appear that they were not stolen unwillingly — probably with much giggling before and after the act'. He was sad, however, that they had to wear rough material. 'It is a base thing that a loutish sheep hide should brush a cheek which knew only the tender touch of a wimple of white linen.'

# THE NORTH DORSET DOWNS

# MILTON ABBAS

Park Farm Museum open
daily 10.00 - dusk

The church and one of the cottages designed by Sir William Chambers

The lack of a focus of settlement right in the heart of Dorset is blamed on the Earl of Dorchester's extreme possessiveness in the 18th century when he obliterated the market town of Milton Abbas, which surrounded the famous abbey. According to the architectural historian, Pevsner, early maps show the town stretching south of the church's east end, with Market Street running away from the precinct, then High Street, Broad Street and many others.

The Dorset historian Treves recalls that the town had a brewery of great renown, many taverns, a grammar school founded in 1521, and over 100 houses in the town proper.

When Joseph Damer, later Earl of Dorchester took possession of the Milton Estates, he found this town just where he wanted to build his mansion, so he razed it to the ground with the typical high-handedness of an 18th-century squire, and rebuilt a village out of sight of his home, about three-quarters of a mile south-east of the abbey. Sir William Chambers built the village in 1780, although Capability Brown had submitted a plan in 1773.

This one-street village is best approached from the Puddletown to Blandford road, the A354, turning left at Milborne St Andrew. Soon the traveller enters a lovely valley in the chalk hills and, as he feels more and more encompassed by the wooded slopes, a large lake appears where swans sometimes battle with waves whipped up by the wind channelled down the corridor of hills.

The almshouses

To the right is the village of Milton Abbas. It is an early example of town planning, with the sturdy thatched cottages, all alike, built on each side of a main road. Each has an expanse of lawn in front of it, and the symmetrical windows in each give them the appearance of doll's houses. Alas, the full beauty of Damer's planning has been lost: originally between each cottage there was a great chestnut tree, but all became diseased and were cut down a few years ago. Halfway up the hill there is a gap in the cottages where the church was built and, right opposite, the almshouses.

James Wyatt's church of St James was built in 1786, but lost its Wyatt character when a new chancel and aisle were added. Unlike the two-up two-down cottages, the almshouses are single-storeyed with accommodation for six and a central communal room. They are a relic of the old town. Built in 1674, they were dismantled and rebuilt in the new village in 1779.

Although the people of Milton Abbas who were uprooted from their ancient homes in those 18th-century days would probably not agree, the village Damer gave them is uniquely beautiful. Times have changed since they were built, and today the cottages are the type of residences that most people would pay a lot of money for.

To see the site of the old town, the explorer must return down the main street of Milton Abbas and at the lake turn right. Trees will cloak his short journey until suddenly the great abbey confronts him. The mansion which Damer built, now a school, does not compare with the architecture of the beautiful abbey. Remember as you walk the lawns — which is permitted during school holidays — that this was once a noisy busy town.

Milton Abbey was founded by Athelstan, the grandson of Alfred the Great, in about AD 938 to house 40 monks. It was enlarged by the Normans. The original building was destroyed by fire in 1309; the present structure, still in an excellent state of preservation, was begun in 1322 but was not completed until within a few years of the dissolution of the monasteries in 1539. The present building displays varied styles. The 101-foot central tower and north transept are Perpendicular, and the choir is early Decorated.

The cloister leaning against the north transept and the Great Hall of Abbot Middleford (1481-1525) are all that is left of the monastic parts. The Hall is now part of the house.

Sir John Tregonwell took over the estate after the Dissolution and the church was allowed to become parochial. Sir Joseph Banks, who had married the heiress of the Tregonwells of Bournemouth, sold Milton in 1752 to Joseph Damer who was married to a daughter of the

Milton Abbey

Duke of Dorset. A year later he was created Lord Milton. It was he who destroyed the old Milton Abbas and rebuilt the village.

A poor restoration in 1789 robbed the church of some of its fittings and it was not until 1865 that Sir Gilbert Scott was commissioned to repair the damage. He left the abbey as we know it today.

The great church is 136 feet long and 61 feet wide. Including the transept, it is over 100 feet wide. There are several notable monuments including a gem by Robert Adam, carved in white marble by Agostino Carlini. It depicts Lady Milton, recumbent with Lord Milton, his head propped up on his arm contemplating her. Treves has a different version. He writes: 'She lies back dead. Her head drops on a pillow on which her loosened hair has tumbled. Her hands fall by her side inert and helpless. The figure is tender, delicate and realistic. By her side her husband, his head resting on his hand. He is assumed to be alive and to be gazing upon her with a look stupified by grief. He wears a bag-wig, sword and pompous robes. He is uncouth, foppish and ridiculous.'

The monastic buildings north of the abbey were converted into a mansion by Sir John Tregonwell, but it was Joseph Damer who employed Sir William Chambers to demolish all but the Abbot's Hall and construct the new mansion in 1771. It was built around four sides of a quadrangle, which makes it perfect for the school which now uses the premises. For a while it was a Faith Healing Centre.

In 1774 Chambers and James Wyatt continued the rebuilding. The former's personality is stamped on the ground floor rooms, and Wyatt's imitation of Adam is to be seen upstairs. Capability Brown landscaped the gardens. The Abbot's Hall, house and grounds are open to the public during school holidays, and many will recognise it as a setting for the television adaptation of the novel *To Serve Them All Our Days* by R.F. Delderfield.

There is a folly a third of a mile to the south-west. Early 19th-century, made like a Gothic chapel front, it is now masked by trees.

St Catherine's Chapel is on a hill 300 yards east of the church. It is Norman and built of flint. From it some unusual steps cut into the turf lead down to the abbey grounds. For the best view of the abbey and house, take the north-west road toward Hilton.

Four miles along the top of the ridge above Milton Abbas is Bulbarrow Hill, one of the highest beaty spots in central Dorset, with breath-taking views of the Blackmoor Vale from its 900-foot elevation.

Half a mile along the road to Bulbarrow, call at the Park Farm Museum to see relics of historic Milton Abbas: old farm implements, brewing artifacts and rural bygones. It has farm animals, a picnic site with panoramic views, a museum shop, a children's play area and a restaurant. There are occasional demonstrations by a blacksmith and thatcher.

The Park Farm Museum

# Cerne Abbas & the Giant

Although Cerne Abbas is one of the country's most ancient and lovely villages, the rude giant on a hillside robs it of some of its dignity, and often causes giggling when explorers arrive.

The Cerne Abbas Giant

So let's deal with this awesome monument first. A colossal figure cut into the chalk of the hillside, he can be seen as you enter Cerne from the Dorchester-Sherborne road (A352). The giant is 180 feet long from head to foot. In his right hand he brandishes a club 120 feet long. His body is outlined in trenches, two feet wide, and his condition has been maintained by regular scourings by local people. Now he belongs to the National Trust.

Because of his resemblance to Hercules, one theory is that he is a Romano-British figure dating from the second century AD. If you seek a closer view, there is a footpath up the hill from the village, leading up through the churchyard.

The giant probably represents a tribal fertility symbol of the prehistoric farming community. Figures like him survive in other parts of southern England, northern Europe and Scandinavia, dating from Bronze Age and early Iron Age civilisations.

There is a local tradition calling the giant by the name of Helith. It stems from the legend of St Augustine's visit to Cerne at the end of the sixth century AD, which mentions that the god Helith was worshipped in Dorset.

Of course there are many local legends surrounding the figure, the most amusing of which concerns the theory that the outline was cut around a real giant sleeping on the hillside after a feast of sheep stolen from the Blackmoor Vale.

Immediately above the giant is the Trendle, a sub-rectangular earthwork terraced into the hillside, with an external bank and ditch. It may have been the site of a temple or shrine associated with the cult of Hercules. Until recently it was the site of village Maypole celebrations, but today the Giant and Trendle are fenced off to prevent erosion.

The village itself, the 'Abbots Cernal' of Hardy's fiction, is a beautiful place which was once the site of a flourishing leather industry. It is said that the local family who made boots for Queen Victoria also made leather hunting suits for Sir Walter Raleigh. Had the railway not bypassed Cerne, it might have become an important industrial centre.

The road past the church is the most interesting part of Cerne, with overhung Tudor residences and, on the corner, a large Georgian house with a shell porch. It is a film-maker's delight and featured in the film of *Tom Jones*.

The church has a high tower with grotesque gargoyles, and a fine pulpit with a canopy dated 1640.

Past the church on the left are the old stocks, and through the graveyard, near Abbey House, is St Augustine's Well — a clear, shallow pool surrounded by trees. Legend says that the saint created the well by striking his staff on the ground, to provide water to baptise converts. Water flows from the spring through the garden of Abbey House and as a stream through the village.

The Abbey House

The fine Abbey House, which is still lived in, is near the ruins of Cerne Abbey. All that remains of the abbey is a handsome gateway and the Pilgrim's House of the 14th century. The abbey was founded in 987 AD in memory of Edmund the Martyr, King of East Anglia, who was killed by the Danes. Canute plundered the church but, on his conversion to Christianity, restored it. The gatehouse is ornamented with coats-of-arms.

When you enter the village from the Dorchester Road, the first building seen is the great barn of the abbey, now partly used as a residence.

At Godmonstone, a small village on the Dorchester side of Cerne Abbas on the A352, be sure and stop at the Smith's Arms. A former blacksmith's forge, it is one of the smallest inns in the country. It is said that King Charles II asked the blacksmith for a drink, and when the man replied that he had no licence to sell ale, the king granted him a licence there and then.

Flint and timber buildings in the village

# MINTERNE HOUSE GARDENS

Gardens open daily
April-Nov
Price guide B

On the A352 road which wends through the valley of the little river Cerne between Dorchester and Sherborne, and nestling among tree-clad slopes, is one of the loveliest gardens in the county. It is a Mecca for those who love the rhododendron.

It is the more interesting because it is the work of generations of the Digby family who have lived at Minterne Magna since 1768 when Admiral The Hon. Robert Digby bought the house and contents from the widow of General Charles Churchill, brother of the famous Duke of Marlborough.

Although Capability Brown laid out the gardens of nearby Sherborne Castle, where the Admiral's elder brother Lord Digby resided, there is no record of him visiting Minterne. Nevertheless the Brown influence is recognisable.

The Admiral planted trees for woodland effect on the bare downland, built bridges, and created lakes and ponds fed by gentle sounding cascades. The trees took a long time to establish themselves but today, over 200 years later, magnificent cedars — one with a girth of 25 feet — and other fine trees make a lovely show. Once the trees were established, laurel, holly, aucuba, box and the rhododendron followed.

Admiral Sir Henry Digby, Nelson's youngest naval captain at Trafalgar, and the nephew of Admiral Robert, continued the work of land-scaping. His son and grandson, the 9th and 10th Lords Digby, started the rhododendron and shrub collection which thrives so well in the greensand of the Minterne valley.

Bamboos were introduced in the 1890s to give shelter for the big-leafed *Rhododendron falconeri* and the early Himalayan introductions *R. thomsonii, campylocarpum, arboreum, strigillosum* and *barbatum*.

Colonel the Lord Digby, an authority on rhododendrons, inherited the gardens in his early twenties and watched the seed collections from China gradually grow into forest trees.

Most visitors with a knowledge of rhododendrons are surprised that, contrary to most ideas, the flowers grow so well under the cover of enormous beech trees. There are at least 350 species of rhododendrons to be seen and at least twice as many hybrids.

The fine mansion built on the site of the old, slightly smaller house is only 80 years old and is believed to be the only large country house designed by architect Leonard Stokes. He created a beautiful sophisticated structure built throughout in the warm-coloured Ham Hill ashlar.

The house is not open to the public, but after you have visited the gardens be sure to spend a while in the peaceful village. Here is a corner of England that still retains a gentle Victorian atmosphere. A village proud of its past, still overawed by the great families who have lived here. It is not spoiled by modern development, and the lovely cottages are covered with climbing roses. Inside the little church of St Andrew the plain cream-coloured walls are covered with ornate memorial tablets to the Churchills, Digbys and Napiers who are all part of Minterne's past. Be careful as you leave the church because the front door opens right on to the main road.

The Churchills were at Minterne prior to the Digbys, having acquired it in the early 1600s. John Churchill was succeeded by the first Sir Winston Churchill, who left it to his son Charles much to the displeasure of his eldest son John, Duke of Marlborough, who having been brought up at Minterne, 'had to make do with Blenheim Palace'. The old Churchill house was demolished in 1900 when it was found to have dry rot.

The present Lord Digby has lived at Minterne all his life with the exception of the war years 1940-5 when it became a naval hospital. In 1957 the west end of the house was converted into six flats while the east was retained as the family home.

# DORCHESTER AND THE FROME VALLEY

# MAIDEN CASTLE

If you tend to be emotional, a visit to Maiden Castle will be an experience rather than a simple pleasure and, when you climb through the ramparts to reach the summit, you may feel that thousands of ghosts are watching.

Two miles south-west of Dorchester, reached by passing Maumbury Rings on the Weymouth road (A354) and turning right opposite Dorchester Cemetery, or a little further south at Winterborne Monkton — the castle on view today dates from the first century BC. Excavation has proved that under the eastern end a Neolithic village of about 3000 BC existed, but the two rings of entrenchment which surrounded it are no longer visible from the ground. Later, but still in this period, a towering mound 60 feet wide and 1,740 feet long was built along the ridge. Although this is no longer visible on the surface, its eastern end lies buried just south of the visible foundations of the Roman temple. Just below these foundations excavators found a human skeleton.

About 1800 BC the hilltop was deserted until the 5th or 4th century BC. At this time the earliest parts of the existing earthworks were built. The builders lived in timber huts. Eventually the population grew, and the enclosure was extended in about 200 BC. It became an Iron Age town defended by a single rampart and ditch, first on the eastern knoll of the ridge, then spreading west with the suburbs being encircled by an extension of the rampart.

In about 100 BC new methods of fortification were imported from overseas, transforming the castle into a massive complex which is not only the finest example of an earthwork in Dorset, but considered to be unsurpassed in Britain. Its multiple defences enclose 47 acres. The castle was in its prime during this period, when about 5000 people lived in crowded huts. They tilled the surrounding land, kept sheep and cattle and favoured a type of dog which was about the size of a foxhound.

In AD 44 the great Roman general Vespasian arrived, commanding the II Legion, and over-whelmed this final stronghold of the Durotriges tribe. After using the fort as a temporary military outpost, the main Roman settlement became established at Dorchester.

Maiden Castle lay dormant for several centuries until nearly 400 AD, when a Romano-British temple was built on the site. It was a square building with a verandah, and you can see the foundations today. When excavated, many objects were found including a small bronze Celtic bull.

A place which had been home to the Celts and a fort for the Romans died in the fifth century AD, and it is no wonder that if you wander alone across the hill on a winter's day you will find it awesome — what Hardy called a 'stupendous ruin'.

In 1934, a large-scale archaeological dig was started, led by Sir Mortimer Wheeler and his wife Tessa Verney-Wheeler, and continued until 1937. Many of the finds can be seen in Dorchester Museum, including some fragments of the temple floor and a bronze plaque of Minerva, as well as gold coins and a ring.

What is left for the explorer is an area half a mile long enclosed by steep earth walls from 60 to 90 feet high. Three or four lines of them encircle the hill; the outer defences are nearly two miles around and complicated earthworks guard the entrances. At the west gate are seven banks through which you can zigzag a way.

Two miles out on the Weymouth road, at the top of the Ridgeway Hill, you can turn right into the old Roman road to the castle, and make the straight descent into Upwey. This road is for walkers only.

# DORCHESTER

It has been said that you only have to scratch the earth anywhere in Dorchester, the county town of Dorset, and you will find a relic of Roman days. But the town — the Casterbridge of the Thomas Hardy novels — is much older than that. It has been in existence since the Iron Age and it was not until AD 70 that the Romans came down from the heights of Maiden Castle and founded their Durnovaria on the banks of the river Frome.

Whichever way you approach Dorchester, the view is pleasant. The main street running east and west is lined with church towers and steeples, and the High Street exits west past the memorial gatehouse of the barracks of the old Dorset Regiment. The gatehouse, with its round towers and an arch between, is now the Dorset Military Museum.

In spite of its early beginnings, Dorchester is now a fairly modern, typical English market town, probably because it has been fought over so often, swept by fire and devastated by plague. To get the feel of its age, the explorer should first go to Maumbury Rings, situated in the Weymouth Avenue (A354) just beyond the brewery. Sit on the bank of this now tidy structure and ponder on its grim past. It was constructed as an earthwork in about 2000 BC, a sacred circle. Excavations have provided proof of its use in fertility rite ceremonies. When the Romans came, they raised the banks of the oval-shaped arena, which is about 200 feet by 160 feet, to form an amphitheatre. The spectators sat on the sloping grass ramparts. Two rings of timber palisades with a space between the inner and outer provided a collecting ring for gladiators waiting their turn to fight. There is evidence of a chamber cut into the chalk, which probably housed the animals used in wild beast shows.

Maumbury Rings

The amphitheatre was abandoned for over a thousand years until 1642 when Parliamentary troops used it as a fortification guarding the road to Weymouth. In the 18th century it was used as a place of execution. The crowds who gathered to watch the public hangings up to the mid-1700s did much to damage the rings. The most ghastly execution to take place there was the burning of the murderess Mary Channing. As 10,000 watched, she was burned to death on the floor of the amphitheatre. Today schoolchildren hold more pleasant parties in this grim place.

On the Bridport road, turn right just before the barracks are reached, and a half-mile journey will bring you to Dorchester's other ancient earthwork, Poundbury. It is a small bi-vallate Iron Age fort of about 15 acres. It was refortified prior to the Roman invasion in the 1st century AD. A vast cemetery between the East Wall and Dorchester was the site of a graveyard in about AD 300-400.

It is difficult to plan an organised walk around a town with such a variety of interesting sites. The old Roman Durnovaria was a walled town enclosing 80 acres, and you can visit the foundations of a small part of the original wall, built in AD 306, at the top of High West Street. It is indicated by a tablet. The line of the walls is marked by the tree-lined walks: Bowling Alley Walk to the west of the Weymouth road, West Walk continuing from that to High West Street, and Colliton Walk from High West Street downhill by the side of Colliton Park. This park is the home of the new County Hall and Crown Court. At its northern end, near the river Frome, is another Dorchester gem. In 1937 the foundations and mosaic floor of a large Roman town house were uncovered. It is unique in Britain, being the only Roman town house of which all the layout can be seen.

Kennington's bronze of Thomas Hardy

At the top of town near the Colliton Park entrance is Eric Kennington's fine bronze memorial to Thomas Hardy, a sitting figure on a base of Portland stone. Walk down High West Street and the Old Crown Court stands gaunt on the left. Inside is the courtroom where the Tolpuddle Martyrs were tried. The restored court and cells are a memorial to these Six Men of Dorset.

St Peter's Church with its great square tower dominates the town centre and beneath it stands the bronze figure of Dorset's other poet and author, William Barnes, but the church pigeons show little respect for him. He looks across the road to the 17th-century house which was the notorious Judge Jeffreys' lodgings in 1685 during his 'Bloody Assize' — the trials

The Old Crown Court - a memorial to the Tolpuddle Martyrs

High West Street

which took place after Monmouth's rebellion. It is now a restaurant. Just below the church is the old Town Hall above the Corn Exchange — built in the mid-19th century of Broadmayne brick and Bath stone. In High East Street look out for the King's Arms Hotel, an early 19th-century building — this is where William Barnes first saw his beloved Julia alight from a stage-coach.

In South Street and Cornhill, the town pump — an obelisk that has become a traffic hazard — stands in the centre of the road. Dated 1784, it replaced an old cupola. Opposite the post office is the minute shopping centre called the Nappers Mite. It was built by Sir Robert Napper in 1616 as an almshouse for ten poor men. Plaques on the walls of 39 and 40 South Street recall that

Napper's Mite

Hardy worked in one as an apprentice to the architect John Hicks, and Barnes had a school in the other. Above the bank, No. 10, is a plaque commemorating that this was the reputed home of Hardy's Mayor of Casterbridge.

Back at the pump, cross the main road to North Square where bull-baiting once took place. Via Colliton Street, you come to Glyde Path Road. Pass the gaunt prison on the site of a former Norman castle, and descend to the river. There you will find a beautiful cottage with an ugly name, Hangman's Cottage, once the home of the executioner. Until 1863, hangings were public and celebrated by a 'Hang Fair'. Here, you can stroll along the river bank — a favourite place for both Hardy and Barnes.

If you now seek refreshment, return to South Street and the Antelope Hotel. An oak-panelled room in this hotel is supposed to be the trial room for Judge Jeffreys' 'Bloody Assize' in 1685. 312 were tried for treasonable sedition and all but 20 received sentence of death.

Hardy fans will wish to see his house. Max Gate is on the A352 road out of Dorchester, but it lies behind a brick wall and is very private. A reproduction of his study is in the Dorchester Museum. If you wish to take a sentimental walk, however, leave the car and take the bridle path opposite his house which rejoins the main road again at Came rectory. Hardy took this walk to watch Barnes' funeral cortege leave the rectory in 1886. Alas, he arrived late, but he wrote a poem about it.

# DORSET COUNTY MUSEUM

Dorset County Museum
open Mon-Fri 10.00-5.00;
Sat 10.00-1.00, 2.00-5.00

Price guide B

Dinosaur Museum open
April-Sept 9.30-5.30 daily;
Oct-Mar 10.00-5.30; closed
Mon

Price guide B

Park your car in a long-stay car park when you visit the Dorset County Museum, because once inside the labyrinth of rooms and corridors you will become so intrigued that you will find it hard to leave. You do not merely view static relics, but see them set out in the colourful scenic settings of their origin.

It is unusual for a county museum to be privately owned, but the Dorset County Museum has been owned and run by the Dorset Natural History and Archaeological Society since its foundation in 1846. Situated in High West Street, Dorchester, its collections encompass local history and geology as well as natural history and archaeology.

Its private status and the generosity of various benefactors has enabled the museum to take some bold decisions — including the building of an extension in 1972 (designed by the architect Michael Brawne), and employing leading museum and exhibition designers to develop the new archaeological gallery. In 1972 the museum was runner-up, with the Ulster Museum, in the Museum of the Year Award.

The new archaeological gallery was opened in 1984. There are many archaeological collections in museums in the British Isles where fine artifacts are displayed, but few which put the finds in their proper context — the burial mounds, village sites, or hillforts where they were found and which are now being threatened by the bulldozer, the plough, and the treasure-hunter. This new gallery is not an Aladdin's cave of spoils amassed by excavators over the past two hundred years; rather it attempts to focus attention on the field monuments — the visible remains of a long-vanished way of life.

Dorset has been in the forefront of scientific archaeology since the days when General Pitt Rivers, whose estate was in the north-east of the county, established the subject as a science. Since then, almost all the leading names in British archaeology have worked in the county. Before the Second World War Sir Mortimer Wheeler, who did so much to popularise archaeology, excavated Maiden Castle. This is perhaps the best-known archaeological site in Britain after Stonehenge, and the finds from it are now superbly displayed in the new gallery.

Within the gallery every type of earthwork left behind by prehistoric man is examined using reconstructions, photographs (from the air and the ground), plans and models. The gallery is not afraid to say 'don't know' many times over to bring home to visitors how many problems are left unsolved from our illiterate past — problems which can only be solved by excavation.

Although the Maiden Castle exhibit forms the core of the gallery, many sites of equal importance are illustrated: recent excavations at the causewayed camp on Hambledon Hill at Iwerne Courtney, the great Neolithic henge monuments at Mount Pleasant in West Stafford, the downland excavations below Hardy's monument at Rowden and Cowleaze in Winterbourne Steepleton, the now destroyed Iron Age and Romano-British farming settlement at Gussage All Saints and the pottery industry around Poole Harbour in Roman times.

Curator Roger Peers, enthusiastic and far-seeing, has created a museum to interest all tastes and full of messages. He displays a model of a house of the Romano-British period. Next to it is the same house in decay, then the earth rings we know today and finally, and with drama, a giant plough is shown cutting through the heart of it.

This emphasises the fact that, although the county is fortunate to have thousands of prehistoric sites, it is not protecting them well

The main hall, with its Victorian cast ironwork

enough. The pace of destruction has increased rather than decreased in recent years because of the scale of road and house building, the advent of deep ploughing, and the fact that farmers are paid handsomely to cultivate the old open downland.

The main Victorian hall of the museum is now occupied principally by the Thomas Hardy and Dorset Worthies Collection. This hall has arches of fine cast ironwork, and was re-decorated in 1966 according to the colour scheme of the original architect; the design and colour of the ironwork was influenced by the Great Exhibition of 1851.

The main item in this hall is a reconstruction of Thomas Hardy's study, as it was when he lived and worked at Max Gate, his house near Dorchester. In the study is the largest collection in the world of Hardy's manuscripts, books from his library and some of his personal possessions.

In the hall itself are items of furniture belonging to Thomas Hardy, and material connected with, among other Dorset Worthies, the poet, scholar and priest William Barnes, Admiral Sir Thomas Masterman Hardy who was Nelson's flag captain at Trafalgar, and Alfred Stevens the Victorian sculptor and artist.

The reconstruction of Hardy's study at Max Gate

By returning to the museum's counter and climbing the main staircase to the top, the visitor will reach the Geology Gallery. On the way, the staircase and landing walls display the fossil remains of extinct reptiles and fishes, occupants of warm seas with covered Dorset 200 to 135 million years ago.

Displays of relics from the more recent past include pottery, costumes, documents and furniture spanning many years, cases of clay pipes dating from 1580 to 1959, tallow candles, a lady's shoe from around Queen Anne's time — which looks very uncomfortable — a case of beautiful beadwork, samplers, and an interesting collection of 'Christening pin-cushions' with welcoming messages to the new infant written out in pins.

# DINOSAUR MUSEUM

The thought of meeting prehistoric monsters sends a shudder down most people's backs, but a visit to the Dinosaur Museum in Icen Way, off the High East Street, may change your ideas. At this, the country's first museum devoted to dinosaurs and their relatives, a model portrays the dinosaur as a sad, lonely animal which you could learn to love.

It is an example of an exciting new kind of display that actively involves the visitor in exploring the mysteries of the past.

The interior of the museum, which is very modern, bright and colourful, contrasts with the exterior of the building — a charming example of the Victorian 'Arts and Crafts' influence. On entering the museum, one encounters a totally new and strange world, a world in which the dinosaurs flourished for over 140 million years, the last becoming extinct nearly 65 million years ago. A visit is a total experience, in which interactive and computerized exhibits blend with fossils, life-size models and a video presentation, to inform and entertain.

One can encounter the 'feelies' and find out what dinosaurs felt like, while another display allows the visitor to mix coloured light to create a dinosaur of different shades, in an effort to answer the question 'what colours were dinosaurs?'. There are interactive displays of all kinds. Exhibits are specially designed to allow them to be frequently changed, which means there will always be new and interesting things to see, no matter how many visits you make.

Getting the measure of a dinosaur

# THOMAS HARDY'S WESSEX

Novelist and poet Thomas Hardy, 1840-1928, not only used Dorset and its people as a background for his novels, but created a fictional region which he called Wessex - a literary ploy which enabled him to write about real people and places. In the heart of 'Wessex' lies the cluster of villages of Stinsford, Higher Bockhampton and Lower Bockhampton, which he called, collectively, 'Mellstock'.

Mellstock, in Hardy's works, is the setting for *Under the Greenwood Tree,* a story of the demise of the local church choir and orchestra as the Vicar falls in love with a pretty young organist who seems to him a much better proposition for leading the services.

It was in this gathering of villages that Hardy was born. His birth-place lies at the end of a quiet lane in Higher Bockhampton; the cottage was built by his grandfather. As Hardy grew up, he saw the building being slowly hemmed in by the forest he wrote about. It is possible, by prior arrangement in writing, to get permission to see the room where he first came into the world, and also the next room where he sat writing about the fictional Wessex of *Under the Greenwood Tree.*

Down the road is Stinsford church, a building which he knew well because his family led the church choir there and where he played the violin, and a building which features in his poetic and narrative works. It was here that Fancy Day won the heart of the new Vicar, and ousted the choir from its stalls with her organ-playing.

Hardy lived for much of his life in the nearby area, latterly at Max Gate on the A352 from Dorchester to Broadmayne, a house he designed himself, and in which he died. And he still lives on in Stinsford, metaphorically speaking, for his heart is buried in the graveyard of that church which was so much part of his life and writings.

Hardy's birthplace at Higher Bockhampton

The names with which Hardy labelled his fictional Wessex are often more beautiful than the actual place names, and the realism of his writing can make it difficult to divorce fact from fiction. So the explorer is lured to many places really believing that the fictional characters lived in these settings.

The centre of Hardy's Wessex is Casterbridge, his invented name for the county town of Dorset, Dorchester. To say that nineteenth-century Dorset is synonymous with Wessex is not really very far from the truth. But Wessex is much more than a geographical area — it is a complete way of life. The people, the countryside, the weather, the seasons, nature and the elements all combine together to perpetuate an era which Hardy saw fast disappearing. Despite this, much of what he wrote about is still evident today.

The King's Arms, Dorchester

Dorchester itself is perhaps the best example. The setting for one of Hardy's most popular novels, *The Mayor of Casterbridge,* much of the town has remained untouched, except to become a little more grimy from the countless motor vehicles which plough through the narrow streets. In High East Street, next to its junction with Friary Lane — that's the road which leads to the prison (the County Gaol in the novels) — is the King's Arms Hotel. It is almost exactly as it was described in the novel, set over a hundred years ago, when Michael Henchard, the hay-trusser who'd sold his wife Susan and baby daughter in a drunken stupor, was seen from outside the inn by that same woman at a banquet some twenty years later. Stand outside the main entrance today during any evening, and glimpse into the same dining room where Susan had that first sight of her lost husband. Then amble out on the road to Bridport, turn around and walk back in the same steps as she and her daughter, Elizabeth-Jane, trod as they entered Casterbridge on their search for father. At the other end of the town, stop and view Grey's Bridge, at the junction of London Road (A35) and Kings Road — a bridge often missed by the casual traveller. It was here that Henchard and other people from all walks of life whiled away their time. Just north of the bridge is the weir-hole where Henchard contemplated suicide.

Weatherbury Upper Farm was the home of Bathsheba, the impetuous heroine of *Far from the Madding Crowd.* Even this is a real place — merely travel along the B3142 from

Puddletown to Piddlehinton and on the right-hand side of the road is Waterston Manor — a place to while away an hour or so to view the delightful gardens. On the way there, look out for Northover Farm, also on the right — that is Little Weatherbury Farm, where lived Mr Boldwood, the bachelor gentleman-farmer, destined to spend his life in gaol for murder.

Winfrith Heath - Egdon Heath in the novels

Anyone who has read the novel must be stricken with shock at the pastoral tragedy of Gabriel Oak's sheepdog chasing the whole flock of sheep over a cliff. That cliff is now somewhat overgrown, but can still be reached by travelling from Dorchester on the A37 and then A356 through Maiden Newton and taking a left turn into the village of Hooke. Pass the church on the right and take the northward path. Gabriel's sheep met their unfortunate end just to the right. A short walk will be required here, and if walking's a pleasure then try following part of Tess's great trek from Emminster (Beaminster) to Flintcombe Ash near Alton Pancras on the B3143 between Piddletrenthide and Buckland Newton. The journey follows a line through Evershed (Evershot) and Minterne Magna. The novel *Tess of the d'Urbervilles* will be needed as a guide.

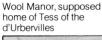

Wool Manor, supposed home of Tess of the d'Urbervilles

Farther south, Hardy had a great affection for Winfrith Heath which lies between the A35 and the A352. He called it Egdon Heath, and the opening paragraphs of *The Return of the Native*, in which it is evoked, stand high on the list of descriptive narratives of English literature. In the novel, the heath dominates the story and the characters in no uncertain way — its ruggedness and wildness infiltrate into those who live on it and traverse it. Now much of the heathland of Hardy's time has been overtaken by the twentieth century. The gorse and stunted trees have, to some extent, been replaced by tank-tracks from the army camp at Bovington, and a dramatic series of concrete buildings forming the nuclear research base at Winfrith, near Wool. But take the A352 from Wareham and branch off just past the roundabout and railway bridge on a minor road signposted to Worgret Heath, stop anywhere for a gentle stroll across the heath, and you will recapture the atmosphere that Hardy himself experienced and which he encapsulated in his writing.

One of the best known Hardy locations is Wool Manor by the banks of the Frome at Wool, where Tess of the d'Urbervilles lived.

Some Dorset towns such as Sherborne and Dorchester have devised local Hardy trails published in booklet form which can be picked up an information bureaux, and a map of Dorset published by Wessex Heritage Tours shows all the Wessex names next to the Dorset equivalents.

It is impossible to travel in Dorset without being close to Hardy's Wessex; it is as much a part of the landscape today as it was a hundred years ago when the author was at his peak.

# WOLVETON HOUSE

Open Sun, Tue, Thur, Bank Hols (daily in Aug) 2.00-6.00
Price guide C

Wolveton, ancient seat of the Jurdains, de Mohuns and Trenchards, hides in meadows less than a mile west of Dorchester, and must be ranked as one of the most beautiful houses in Dorset. It is on the A352 near the point where the little river Cerne joins the Frome. Its name is of Saxon origin, and it is fair to assume that a house has stood there since those days.

The south front

The Trenchards came from Hampshire in 1480 and became a leading Dorset family. They built a compact courtyard house early in the 16th century, and enlarged it about 50 years later. The enlargement remains almost intact but, sadly, only the gatehouse and south-west corner of the original house, built by Sir Thomas Trenchard, remains. Building additions took place in the 17th, 18th and 19th centuries.

The east-facing gatehouse conveys the fact that, in its entirety, Wolveton must have been a beautiful and romantic building. Thomas Hardy described Wolveton in his *A Group of Noble Dames* as an ivied manor house, flanked by battlemented towers, more than usually distinguished by the size of the mullioned windows. In recent years, the ivy has been removed to reveal the beauty of the stonework and the irregular towers built of coursed limestone and rubble.

The massive gatehouse

The house became neglected at the end of the 18th century, and was finally sold to the Hennings of Dorchester. In 1862, another kinsman, W.H.P. Weston, saved it from complete ruin and, in recent years, it came into the hands of the present ower, Captain Thimbleby, who is connected with the Trenchard family.

The romantic past of Wolveton is told in countless stories — probably the most famous being the arrival of Archduke Philip of Austria and his Spanish wife Joanna, the daughter and heiress of Ferdinand of Castile and Isabella of Aragon.

In 1506, the couple were on their way from the Netherlands to claim the throne of Castile, when they were caught in a terrible storm at Weymouth. Fearing she would die, Joanna dressed in her finest robes so that her body would be given a noblewoman's funeral. The boat made Weymouth safely and Sir Thomas Trenchard rode down and took the royal couple to Wolveton House. There was a language difficulty and Sir Thomas sent for his young kinsman, John Russell, who lived near Bridport, to act as interpreter. When later they were invited to Windsor, John accompanied them and made such an impression at court that it eventually won him an earldom. He served three kings and a queen, and his successor became the first Duke of Bedford.

During the time of Sir Thomas Trenchard in the 16th century, a visiting judge came to dine. In the middle of the meal he left abruptly. He told his marshal that he had seen the figure of a woman with her throat cut behind Lady Trenchard's chair. A messenger overtook his coach to report that Lady Trenchard had committed suicide.

A cider press in one of the outbuildings

A less tragic ghost story concerns the wager of a member of the family, who drove a horse and carriage to the top of the Great Stairs. His ghost is, they say, frequently seen making the descent.

The house, with its unique stone staircase of 1580 and Great Hall with panels of monkeys in human dress carved in 1500, and the gardens — which although overgrown still retain their 16th-century form — are well worth exploration. Captain and Mrs Thimbleby welcome you to their home.

# ATHELHAMPTON HALL

Open 18 April - 14 Oct
Wed, Thur, Sun (also Mon-
Tue in Aug) 2.00-6.00

Athelhampton Hall, hiding itself from the main A35 Dorchester-Poole road midway between Puddletown and Tolpuddle, is a magnificent relic of the Dorset of bygone years. Arriving through the trees, the explorer is confronted with a house of breathtaking beauty. The Dorset historian Treves went further when he wrote: 'it is without question the most picturesque house in the county.' Approaching from the south on a sunny day, the late Perpendicular hall with its porch and oriel, and the later parlour wing, make a grand show. The older part is all of creamy limestone from Portesham, but later parts have golden Ham Hill stone dressing against the cream walls.

The house was built in the late 15th century, and was the home of the Martin family for 400 years, although the family — descended from Martin of Tours who came over with the Conqueror — had lived at Athelhampton since the early part of the 13th century.

The Great Chamber

The present Athelhampton was built for Sir William Martin, a Lord Mayor of London. Finance was no problem and he demanded the best building money could buy for his family home. What is called the new wing was added in the time of Henry VII. The explorer is denied the sight of the gatehouse with its two floors, great oriel window and gabled roof because it was pulled down in 1862; the chapel went at the same time.

You can see the grand Banqueting Hall with its open oak roof and a lovely oriel window. The north end of the hall leads into the 'new wing' — new in the 16th century.

Here is the King's Ante-room and the Parlour. An oak staircase leads to the Long Gallery Library above. The interesting newel staircase has its solid wooden blocks let into the stonework. There are elaborate plaster ceilings, and a secret stair is concealed in the thickness of the walls. The Oratory and the State Bedroom are in a wing south of the Great Hall which, with another wing, forms an inner courtyard.

The house has rich panelling, 15th-century doors and fine furniture. Some of the windows have the original painted glass.

Yew pyramids in the gardens

Over the front porch is a small bedchamber surmounted by battlements, and the wing to the left of the entrance has powerful buttresses, supporting walls incorporating Gothic windows of sturdy proportions.

Set away from the rambling house, with its irregular rooftops and countless dormers, is an attractive circular dovecote built of rubble stone, buttressed and with a conical roof.

The three separate enclosed gardens are a feature of this lovely house, laid out to the south-east of the building. One has an exceptionally pretty circular enclosure with a cresting of obelisks.

Those who love gardens are in for a feast at Athelhampton. The 25-foot yew pyramids are remarkable and the great court has a water terrace reminiscent of the Villa d'Este. The gardens are mentioned by Jane Austen and Gertrude Jekyll, and the Octagon, with its lime cloister, was the prototype for New Palace Yard, Westminster.

The story of the Martin family had a sad ending when Nicholas, the last of the line, was laid to rest in 1595. He was the last of this gallant company of Dorset squires because he had four daughters but no son, and we must imagine his sadness as he sat in these beautiful gardens watching his daughters play, and longing for a son who would carry on the family name.

It was not to be, and when he was buried, this man who had everything he needed except a son had this inscribed on his tomb: 'Nicholas ye first and Martyn ye last. Goodnight Nicholas.' The inscription is no longer decipherable.

Do not expect to see the tomb in the church of St John in Athelhampton. This very ordinary edifice of the 1860s is of little interest except perhaps for its stone pulpit projecting from the wall. Nicholas Martin's last resting place is in Puddletown church which has Norman origins.

# TOLPUDDLE AND THE MARTYRS' MUSEUM

Under the Martyrs' Tree

Museum open 9.00-dusk
Admission free

It is a tragedy that the planners widened and levelled the fast main A35 road through Tolpuddle instead of bypassing one of the country's most famous villages. It should have been left in its rural state, as a peaceful memorial to the heroic early days of trade unionism, where visitors from all over the world could come to pay homage to the Six Men of Dorset.

The six early 19th-century farm labourers were not fighting for a rise in pay, but to stop the reduction in their annual wages from nine to seven shillings in three years. When it was decided to make a further cut to six shillings, the farm labourers turned to the Grand National Consolidated Trades Union for help and advice. As a result, The Friendly Society of Agricultural Workers was formed at Tolpuddle. Employers and magistrates took fright and appealed to the Home Secretary, Lord Melbourne. The upshot was that the leader George Loveless — a staunch Wesleyan and local preacher on the Weymouth circuit — and five others were arrested in February 1834, imprisoned at Dorchester and, in March, were sentenced to seven year's transportation. They became known as the Tolpuddle Martyrs.

Before passing sentence on the Tolpuddle men, the judge asked if the defendants had anything to say. Thereupon George Loveless handed him a paper on which he had written: 'My Lord, if we have violated any law, it was not done intentionally; we have injured no man's reputation, character, person or property; we are uniting together to preserve ourselves, our wives and our children, from utter degradation and starvation. We challenge any man, or number of men, to prove that we have acted, or intended to act, different from the above statement'.

In passing sentence, the judge said: 'The object of all legal punishment is not altogether with a view of operating on the offenders themselves, it is also for the sake of offering an example and warning and, accordingly, the offence of which you have been convicted, after evidence that was perfectly satisfactory, the crime, to a conviction of which that evidence has led, is of that description that the security of the country and the maintenance of the laws of which the welfare of this country depends, make it necessary for me to pass on you the sentence required by those laws'.

No wonder the six were confused, but they were soon on their way to serve their sentences. Thomas Stanfield and his son John, James Brine, James Hammett and the younger Loveless, sailed from Plymouth on the convict ship Surrey bound for New South Wales. George, who had been ill after the trial, followed in another ship and was landed in Tasmania. The men had harrowing experiences in the chain gangs.

Meanwhile, there was a public outcry and, in London, a public meeting was attended by 10,000 people and a petition bearing over 800,000 names was presented to Parliament. After a long battle, all the men received a free pardon.

Entering Tolpuddle from the east, the memorial gate on the Methodist Chapel can be seen on the left. It was unveiled in 1912 by the Rt. Hon. Arthur Henderson, a Labour leader, and — like the Six — a staunch Methodist. The chapel the Martyrs attended is a ruin on the other side of the road next to Thomas Stanfield's cottage. At the heart of the village is the Martyrs' Tree where they held their meetings. A memorial seat is on the green. In the churchyard is the grave of James Hammett. As you leave the village, the six memorial cottages are on the right. In their midst is the museum, mainly displaying prints and photographs telling the history of agricultural trade unionism with particular references to Tolpuddle.

Tolpuddle Church, and the Museum

# CLOUDS HILL

Open April-Sept, Wed, Thur
Fri, Sun 2.00-5.00;
Oct-Mar, Sun 1.00-4.00
Price guide C

In the heart of Hardy's great heath, surrounded by woodland and swathed by rhododendron bushes, stands a little insignificant cottage just over a mile from Moreton and within earshot of the rumbling tanks on the training grounds of the Royal Armoured Corps at Bovington. It is a humble home, yet it is now practically a shrine to one of the strangest and most colourful heroes in the history of Britain, having been the simple retirement place of Col. T.E. Lawrence, Lawrence of Arabia.

The cottage where Lawrence found seclusion

The National Trust looks after the cottage, which has the simple words 'Nothing Matters' written in Greek over the door. Lawrence bought it when, after years of living amongst international intrigue and having been the confidant of famous men, he sought a simpler life and a different identity as Aircraftsman Shaw, T.E. in the RAF. The cottage is still furnished with his Spartan requirements: some chairs, a table and a couch. Yet the guest room was modernistically decorated with aluminium wallpaper and fenders of shining stainless steel.

Also in the cottage are the sleeping bags he and his secretary used, marked Meum and Tuum, meaning mine and thine. In the music room, upstairs, is a collection of 800 records and his old gramophone. Here, in his last days, in the peace of this woodland, he would listen to Beethoven, Mozart and Schubert.

Because of the nature of his work, less is known about him than other great heroes such as Nelson, Wellington or Drake, and he refused all honours or distinctions, dismissing it all by saying he had performed his appointed task and there was no reason for making a fuss about it. But what of that task?

He was a scholar, knew many languages, and was knowledgeable about the Near East. He became a distinguished archaeologist in Syria, Palestine and Arabia. The First World War found him acting as interpreter in the Department of Intelligence (Near East Forces), but within a short time his character and personality raised him to the heights of leadership.

Almost single-handed, he engineered a revolt of the Arab tribes against the occupying Turkish forces. The undisciplined Arabs, many of them brigands and nomads, accepted him as a universally-acknowledged chieftain, and although not of their race or religion he united them against their common enemy and led them to victory. His consolidation of the Arab Forces made possible Lord Allenby's triumph in Palestine and the rout of the Turkish Army.

After the war, this man who had lived as a desert Arab, and who had walked with politicians and high ranking Army officers, came home and joined the RAF in the lowest ranks. His motives have never been fully understood, and mystery continued to surround him until the day he died. Of his Arab adventures he wrote *The Seven Pillars of Wisdom* and, later, a controversial book on the RAF called *The Mint*.

He died as he lived, in a blaze of publicity. His death, in 1935, was caused by his love of fast motorcycles. Travelling at great speed along the straight road to Moreton to send a telegram, he mysteriously crashed. To this day, no satisfactory answer has been given as to how it happened, but rumour and conjecture surrounds him in death as it did in life.

Lawrence's grave in Moreton Churchyard

May was in all its magnificence when they brought his body to Moreton Church at the age of 47, and many famous people, including the King of Iraq, walked behind his coffin. A simple posy of lilac and forget-me-nots was laid on the grave, which was later marked with a primitive cross in wood inscribed "To the dear memory of T.E. Lawrence, Fellow of All Souls College, Oxford; born 16th August 1888; died 19th May 1935. 'The hour is coming and now is when the dead shall hear the voice of the Son of God' ". At the foot of the grave is a carved book inscribed 'Dominus Illuminatio Mea' (the Lord is my light).

While at Moreton, take a look at the grave of the son of a Red Indian Chieftain known as Prince Clarence. He came from the Mosquito Territory, part of Nicaragua. He died whilst at school in England and you can look at a grave that no member of his family has seen.

114

# THE TANK MUSEUM

Open daily (except at Christmas) 10.00-5.00
Price guide C

The first armoured tanks were thoroughly tested on the sacred sand of Hardy's blasted heath, but when the first tank went into battle in 1916, Lord Kitchener pointed a finger of scorn. 'A pretty mechanical toy' he observed, and other top generals supported him.

It was Winston Churchill who, seeing the potential of the new weapon, formed a 'Landship Committee'. Eventually the tanks went into action on 16th September 1916 and, by August 1917, were proving their value. Tanks won a decisive battle in August 1918 at Amiens, making a gap 11 miles wide through the German lines.

At Bovington Camp, near Wool, a museum presents a history of armour. Over the past 60 years the collection has increased in size until it must now rate as one of the finest and most comprehensive collections of Armoured Fighting Vehicles in the world.

The museum began at the end of the Great War, when Tank Corps units began to reduce in strength on general demobilisation. Large numbers of tanks were accumulated on heathland north of Bovington Camp waiting to be scrapped. From this tank park some 26 vehicles, comprising every in-service and experimental model, were collected and moved to a half-acre site and fenced off. These vehicles were the beginnings of the Tank Museum.

In 1923, Rudyard Kipling expressed his disappointment that more was not being done to preserve these unique machines and, in 1924, a start was made by housing a selection of them in an open-sided shed. These included both 'Little Willie' and 'Mother'. The following year an equipment store was taken over to house souvenirs and relics, and the embryo museum was considerably enlarged in 1928.

During the Second World War a number of museum tanks saw 'active service' during the invasion scare of 1940, being used for local defence schemes. 'Little Willie', for example, guarded the approaches to Bovington and later became a strong-point on a Gloucestershire airfield. The Mark V was stationed on the Wareham Road. This proved a blessing in disguise, because they were thus saved from the scrapyard which destroyed many irreplaceable relics, including 'Mother'.

After the war, the museum re-opened and in 1951 the collection was greatly increased by the addition of a large number of Allied and Foreign AFVs (armoured fighting vehicles) which had been accumulated during the war. These included a splendid collection of German vehicles, such as the Tiger I which is now one of the most popular exhibits in the museum. Stories abound that the tank is haunted by a spectre called 'Herman the German'. However, its history has been traced fairly carefully, and we know this to be untrue. It was the first Tiger to be taken almost complete by the British in Tunisia.

The Tank Museum houses both the Royal Tank Regiment Museum as well as collections of Royal Armoured Corps exhibits and there are now over 150 AFVs on display inside and outside the museum premises. The exhibition covers the complete historical and technical development of the armoured fighting vehicle from 1915 to modern times. More modern exhibits include a Chieftain, Scorpion, Leopard I, Spahpanzer, AMX 13, Panhard EBR and T54. One of the most interesting recent additions is an ex-Argentinian AML90, captured in the Falklands. Vehicles form

only a part of the collection and they are well supported by models, displays, sectionalised engines and other memorabilia from all theatres of war.

The museum's Diamond Jubilee ocurred in 1983, and a £1 million appeal was launched in order to modernise and improve the museum's facilities. So far the appeal has enabled the museum to build a new entry block, containing a self-service shop, offices and library, a cafeteria and cinema/seminar complex. As the proceeds of the appeal build up, they will finance the remainder of the programme which includes an extra covered exhibition hall, a workshop and a conservation area. The museum has recently greatly enlarged car park and coach park, so that there is plenty of room for visitors, while the large picnic area which adjoins it is much frequented in the summertime.

Bovington Camp is the 'home' of the Royal Armoured Corps Centre, so there are at times also opportunities to see tanks and armoured cars training and on the live firing ranges at Lulworth Camp. Once a year, on the last Sunday in July, the RAC Centre throws its gates open to the public, with mobility displays and mock battles.

# CRANBORNE CHASE, BLANDFORD, AND WIMBORNE

Ashmore
Woodcutts
Sixpenny Handley
CRANBORNE CHASE
Hinton St. Mary
Sturminster Newton
Hambledon Hill
Tarrant Hinton
Cranborne
Has Hill
Pimperne
Knowlton
Blandford Forum
Horton
Badbury Rings
Kingston Lacy
Wimborne Minster
Merley Bird Gardens

○ Ancient Monument.
△ Steep Hill.
⋯⋯ Dorset Cursus

# THE EASTERN HILLS: HOD AND HAMBLEDON

The eastern hills, celebrated by the poet William Barnes, and standing at the western extremity of Cranborne Chase, were to him the backcloth of his beautiful beloved Blackmoor Vale.

> And yonder down beneath us crawls
> The Stour towards the Eastern Hills,
> To drive by many foaming falls
> The mossy wheels of many mills.

A man of peace, he may not have considered that these hills were once the scene of war and awful bloodshed over the long period of man's habitation.

As hills are measured, they are mere pimples. Hambledon is not much over 600 feet and Hod is a hundred feet less, yet an authority on hillforts has described them — along with the other formidable Dorset multi-rampart fortresses Maiden Castle and Badbury Rings — as being amongst the most spectacular of English prehistoric earthworks, monuments to military engineering and tribal organisation. In their early days we must imagine Hod and Hambledon not green and rounded as Barnes knew them, but with their tops bare chalk gleaming white, crowned by defensive palisades. The great Roman general, Vespasian, sweeping west across the country in AD 43 during the conquest of Britain, had cause to remember their strength.

You arrive via the A350 road from Blandford. As you enter Stourpaine, Hod Hill forms the background to your view. Continue towards Shaftesbury, twisting through a mile of bends until a left-hand turning directs you to Shroton, in the lee of Hambledon Hill. An easier climb to the summit can be made from nearby Childe Okeford; the path is a few yards north of a lay-by and leads through beeches. A half mile further south-east is another approach through a dark yew wood. Like most hillforts, Hambledon is a lonely yet beautiful place to visit with magnificent views of the vale and Cranborne Chase.

Too steep a climb for most visitors and with its sides too difficult to plough, it is a natural refuge for butterflies and small birds. The exquisite marbled white butterfly is common here. Hambledon Hill has been designated a grade one Site of Special Scientific Interest and is the foremost chalk downland site for flora and fauna in the south.

A Neolithic causewayed camp (about 2500 BC), traces of which are almost ploughed out, lies on the hill which also contains the remains of an Iron Age fort.

Shroton Church, where the clubmen were locked up

But it is two later historical events which have brought fame to Hambledon. The summer of 1645, during the Civil War, was the climax of the clubmen's rebellion. For the benefit of the explorer who has not heard of the clubmen, they were a kind of citizens' army — formed by countrymen, churchmen and wealthy landowners who had no interest in the fortunes of Royalists or Parliamentarians, but were fed up with their lands being ruined and crops spoiled by the fighting. It is strange that Dorset should have been the centre of this organisation, despite that fact that it was not at the heart of the conflict. However, such gentry as the Earl of Salisbury at Cranborne, and Colonel Weld at Lulworth each had their houses sacked, and the estates of the Arundels, Ashley Coopers and Digbys suffered pillaging by soldiers. So in May 1645 a meeting of about

Hambledon Hill, looking north towards Shaftesbury

4000 tradesmen and others armed with clubs, billhooks, pitchforks and swords assembled on Cranborne Chase, and an association was formed. They sent a petition to both King and Parliament entitled the Humble Petition of the Distressed Inhabitants of the County of Dorset, demanding an end to the fighting and a peaceful settlement of the Civil War.

General Wolfe (1729-1759) trained his troops at Hambledon Hill in preparation for the Battle of the Plains of Abraham in Quebec (1759), where his victory ended French rule in Canada.

Hod Hill has earthworks of similar vintage to Hambledon, and there are traces of a Roman camp, AD 45-63, in the north-west corner.

The view north from Hod Hill

The clubmen's aims were summed up thus: 'If you offer to plunder or take our cattle, be assured we will give you battle'. Their attacks at Sturminster, Lyme and Sherborne were merely a nuisance when compared to the serious fighting and neither side took them seriously. Eventually Sir John Fairfax instructed Cromwell to deal with them personally. He 'got around the table' with some of them at Shaftesbury and convinced them that their lands would not be touched, so that group went home happy. Not so the two thousand who had entrenched themselves on Hambledon Hill, led by the Rev. Thomas Bravell of Compton Abbas. He would not heed Cromwell's pleas to surrender and a fierce battle ensued. Cromwell's men made short work of the clubmen who were scattered, many sliding down the hillside on their backsides. Three hundred of them, including four clergymen, were locked up all night in Shroton church and, on release next morning, went home — having had enough.

The double rampart of Hod Hill

Recent investigations have proved that it is one of the most interesting sites in England for its archaeology and botany.

The county magazine *Dorset*, and its editor Rodney Legg have long been concerned with Hod Hill. The magazine carried the story of the damage done when Hod was so little regarded that the 2500-year-old causewayed camp was ploughed up to prevent crop damage by its rabbits and other vermin during the last war. The ploughing, however, led to some amazing finds including the handle of a religious offertory bowl, one of the most important Celtic artifacts ever found in Britain, and a small bronze head from a warrior's helmet. The handle, dedicated to the god Nodons, was cast on the hill.

According to Rodney Legg, 'The finds take the pre-Roman invasion history of Hod Hill out of the mists of pagan barbarianism and into a world of intellectual and artistic advancement we never knew existed'.

When it was conquered by the Romans in AD 44, Hod Hill entered an even more civilised phase. The Roman fort had military headquarters, cavalry barracks, a hospital and other buildings.

The hillfort has a double line of ramparts, strongest where the approach is easiest. At one point the inner entrenchment rises, even now, to a height of 41 feet above the ditch.

Now Hod — which mean quiet — can be appreciated for its remote beauty and wealth of natural history. It has now been taken under the wing of the National Trust, to join Hambledon which was acquired earlier, and Hod's 67 acres will be safe from development by commercial farming.

# BLANDFORD FORUM

Royal Signals Museum open
Mon-Fri 9.00-1.00; 2.00-4.30
Admission free

The Georgian Church

Blandford grew up at an important crossing place of the Stour and early visitors to it included King John in 1216. By 1305, it was sufficiently important to send two members to Parliament, whilst its market was one of the major ones in Dorset. In 1307 a grant was given by Edward I to Henry de Lacy, Earl of Lincoln, who was Lord of the Manor of Blandford, to enable him to hold a fair twice a year at his *ville* of Blandford. The Manor later passed to Henry, Duke of Lancaster and became part of the Duchy of Lancaster in 1399 on his becoming King Henry IV.

By the time of the first Elizabeth, the town's markets and fairs had achieved considerable fame and Blandford, as well as being home to several wealthy residents, had its own grammar school and was the venue of assizes. Its status as a borough, recognised from early medieval times, was confirmed by a Charter of Incorporation granted by James I in 1605.

Despite suffering from serious fires in the 16th, 17th and early 18th centuries, Blandford continued to prosper and Defoe, writing in 1724, called it a 'handsome, well built town, but chiefly famous for making the finest bone lace in England.'

Blandford owes its countenance of ornate Georgian edifices to a coincidence: the fact that when a great fire devastated it in 1731 the Bastard family, Thomas and his sons John and William, established architects and builders, were on hand to create a new townscape. So Blandford, an attractive market town on the banks of the Stour and surrounded by the rolling chalk downs, is one of the few towns in England where all the buildings at its centre are of the same date, and from the same drawing board.

John and William Bastard were not only civic dignitaries; they had lost their own properties in the fire which started in a tallow chandler's shop and spread as far as Blandford St Mary, west of the town bridge.

With the money which flowed in from all over the country, including £1000 from George II, the Bastard brothers designed and built the new church (a great favourite with Sir John Betjeman), the Town Hall, Grammar School, and many houses which remain unchanged today. A perambulation is well worthwhile but first it is better to know something of the town's historical background.

The explorer can leave his car at the car park by the Stour and stand for a while on the beautiful bridge. High up on the tree-covered south bank, Bryanston School — formerly the home of Lord Portman — hides itself within the great park. As you walk into town, the Georgian facades greet you and, as a preview, a magnificent group of 18th-century frontages are on the left.

Ignore the Market Square and continue up Salisbury Street to note the gateway of the old Anchor Inn under an oriel window. On the walls are ladder brackets for use in case of fire. Further along is No. 38, now a shop, but a plaque indicates that this was the home of Alfred Stevens, the well known sculptor and painter, born in 1818. Orpen described him as being 'the most thoroughly educated artist the country has seen'. His most famous work was the Wellington Monument in St Paul's. Walk higher up the street and admire the Ryves Almshouses, one of the few buildings to survive the great fire. It was built in 1682 and gave accommodation for ten poor persons.

Ryves Almshouses

Retrace your steps to the road junction and turn left into the Plocks, once the enclosure for sheep waiting for the market. Coupar House, at the top of Church Lane, is considered to be one of the grandest houses in Blandford. It stands opposite Lime Tree House, another exquisite architectural gem. Nearby in the Tabernacle, now a car park, is the oak tree planted to commemorate the granting of a Royal Charter to the borough in 1605.

Lime Tree House

Follow through to The Close and to The Old House — like the Almshouses, it was spared by the fire, at which time it was the home of a German doctor who rendered valiant service to the injured. It is an interesting residence with a steeply pitched roof and clustered chimneys. Dorset Street and Orchard Street also have fine examples of 19th-century terraced houses.

In the Market Square, the Town Hall and church complement each other and on the north and south sides of the Market Place, the full richness of the Bastards' work can be observed.

The Town Pump, and the museum entrance between the houses of the Bastard brothers

The Town Hall, with its open entrance of square pillars and rounded arches with splendid lanterns, is entered through the Shambles (slaughter house) with the Corn Exchange beyond; the civic offices are on the first floor. The market scene is dominated by the church with its tall square tower and cupola. Outside is the monument to the fire. It takes the form of an ornate town pump with Doric columns supporting an entablature and triangular pediment. John Bastard designed it, and its date, 1760, would seem to mark the end of the rebuilding. It is inscribed 'In Grateful Acknowledgment of the DIVINE MERCY, that has raised this town, like the PHOENIX from its ashes, to its present beautiful and flourishing state'. It was a case of shutting the door after the horse had fled because the principal use of the pump was to supply a head of water in the event of any future fire.

The Old Coach House Museum opened at Bere's Yard in 1984 — like all good museums, is in a building of some historic interest. The workshops and stables of the Bastard brothers has been adapted for the museum's use. It is entered through a coaching gateway which separates the Bastard's two houses. Bere's Yard is right opposite the church.

The Honorary Curator, Mr Ben Cox, heads an enthusiastic team. It is planned to restrict the collections to items directly concerned with the life, industry and culture of Blandford, and the immediate district on which it depends for its support economically.

It is presenting a collection of prehistoric and Romano-British material, mostly on loan from the county museum, together with items of medieval origin and from the 17th, 18th and 19th centuries.

Two miles north-east of the town is a permanent army camp on a site where in the past both Wolfe and Wellington reviewed their troops. It is the home of the Royal Signal Corps Museum, which is open to the public to show visitors the history and achievements of the Corps.

Communications are the business of the Royal Signal Corps, and on the forecourt is a huge cable-wagon which would have been drawn by a six-horse team, and whose purpose was to lay field-cable.

Triumph motor-cycles which were used for both despatch-carrying and for team display begin the exhibition, and there are other forms of transport, primitive and up-to-date. There are pack-saddles and harness, and photos show some of the animals used by the corps in odd corners of the world — including a yak and an elephant! There is a sad tale too of a pigeon (which you can see stuffed) which was shot in flight while on a 'mission', but which struggled home to deliver its message, and died shortly afterwards of its wounds.

For the technical, there is a variety of complicated equipment — a Marconi wireless-sender, telewriter, automatic transmitters with perforated tapes, hand generators, portable switchboards, and the first telegraph instrument to be used in battle in the Crimea in 1855. There is also an original report of a major victory sent to the Queen in 1882.

# CRANBORNE CHASE

The Cranborne Chase, hunting ground of royalty, stretching along the chalk hills on the Dorset border, is more than a place of local Dorset history — it is an important part of our national heritage. The plough and woodman's axe have changed much of the wild nature of the 100-square-mile Chase, but here and there you will find little woods which can have changed little since its history began. Thomas Hardy described Cranborne Chase as 'a truly venerable tract of forest land, one of the few remaining woodlands in England of undoubted primeval date, wherein druidical mistletoe is still found on aged oaks and where enormous yew trees, not planted by the hand of man, grow as they had grown when they were pollarded for bows'.

There was a time when the north boundary of the Chase extended from Shaftesbury to Salisbury, and it had for its other boundaries the Stour and the Avon rivers. The perimeter was over 80 miles long and, through the centre of it, ran the Roman road from Old Sarum to Exeter.

The creatures hunted were mainly fallow deer. Red deer were introduced but did not fare well on the chalklands. As recently as 1828, there were about 12,000 head of deer running wild.

To learn something of the Chase's old days, go to Woodyates on the A354 from Blandford. Here, where the downs of Dorset, Hampshire and Wiltshire meet, there was a pass which signalled the entry into Dorset, once the site of a city, but all that has gone. Woodyates now has no church or inn and is little more than a hamlet.

When you look down from the slopes and see the cars speeding to Salisbury, remember that through this pass a succession of races through uncountable centuries entered Dorset. It is now a remote spot surrounded by the graves of the warriors who once lived there. Roman, Saxon and Dane fought in this pass. The Woodyates Inn became a famous staging post later and it was here that the Duke of Monmouth, fleeing for his life after the Battle of Sedgemoor, abandoned his horse and — dressing as a shepherd boy — set out to reach the coast on foot. A few days later he was captured at Horton.

Leave this grim corner of Dorset, surrounded by the great dykes Ackling, Bockerley and Grims, and follow the A354 west to Sixpenny Handley — that strangely named village which was formerly two Saxon Hundreds, Sexpenne and Hanlege, united 600 years ago. This is another ancient place on the Chase which has produced relics of Neolithic hunters and Iron Age man. It was devastated by fire in 1892, rendering 100 of the inhabitants homeless.

Beef cattle grazing on the Chase

The B3081, on which you are now travelling, leads to Woodcutts — probably the most interesting village on the Chase. 'The cottages in the woods' is the derivation of its name but the Woodcutts you will see — a pleasant hamlet with cottages built around neat commonland — bears no resemblance to the ancient village, the remains of which are close at hand. This was inhabited by men who lived there from the Iron Age and through the Roman period until the site's abandonment about AD 370.

A high downland settlement, it was occupied just prior to the Roman conquest as a single farmstead. The Romano-British village built later was excavated by General Pitt-Rivers before the turn of the century. Bracelets, brooches and pottery were among his finds. The little townlet was apparently divided into separate quarters and had three well-marked entrances; the General reconstructed the village as a large model which can now be seen in Salisbury Museum.

The little 13th-century church at Chalbury

Just out of Woodcutts, turn left at a minor road to backtrack to Farnham, once the home of General Pitt-Rivers' famous museum. This is now closed, but the pretty village is worth a visit before stopping at Larmer Tree. This is the place where King John, who held the hunting rights in the Middle Ages, met his huntsmen when he stayed at nearby Tollard Royal. The old wych elm has long since died, but its stump can be seen behind protective railings.

The unique gardens at Larmer Tree are sometimes open to the public. If they are you will see an amazing collection of structures grouped around a field. There is Boehm's statue of 'The Hunter of Early Days' — a Celt mounted on a shaggy pony — as well as houses in the style of Eastern lands, a bandstand and an open-air theatre. A strange collection to find deep in the heart of Dorset.

Having seen Larmer Tree, climb the hill to Ashmore, passing a road lined by green common land. Here, in spring, bluebells cluster around the roots of great shady trees, and all about is a patchwork of fields of green and gold and the occasional vivid yellow of oilseed rape.

Ashmore stands on the hill which is the boundary of Dorset, as beautiful and peaceful a village as you will see anywhere in the county. Lovely buildings in stone are reflected in a large pond where ducks chatter and play, and where artists sit on the pond edge to record the scene. From Ashmore the views of the Chase are breathtaking. Below is Stubhampton Bottom, one of the last remnants of the primeval forest. Once all the Chase was like this — wild and untamed — until the farmers took over. That was back in the days when King John hunted here, to be followed by a succession of monarchs until James I, from whom the Chase passed to the Earls of Shaftesbury and then to the Pitt-Rivers family.

Cranborne Chase has had many facets. Even the great smuggler, Gulliver, had an HQ at Sixpenny Handley. Perhaps he had a market for the deer.

# THE DORSET CURSUS

Long barrows mark one end of the cursus

A cursus, for the benefit of explorers who may be puzzled, is defined as a drive or avenue or possibly a racecourse. The Dorset cursus is situated between long barrows near Gussage St Michael and the Bokerley Dyke on the county border near Pentridge, and is thought to have been a processional way in Neolithic times.

Six miles out of Blandford on the A354 road turn right at the Farnham-Ringwood crossroads. Half a mile along the Ringwood road the long barrows can be seen on your left. The cursus, marked by two parallel banks ninety yards apart, is over six miles long. About half-way along its course it is cut across by the Roman road Ackling Dyke. It ends just past Pentridge, in a squared earthwork.

One of the best-preserved sections, and the easiest for the explorer to find, is at Bottlebrush Down where it crosses the B3081.

# CRANBORNE MANOR GARDENS

Garden open first Sat and Sun of each month, April-Oct

Garden Centre open daily 2.00-5.00

The best way to approach Cranborne is by the B3078 road from Wimborne which follows the little river Allen and gives the explorer views of some of the county's richest agricultural land.

Alone on a crossroads stands the Horton Inn, and nearby is Horton Tower, a folly built by Humphry Sturt in 1700. From the top of the 120-foot tower he could spot deer on the land around.

Horton Tower

Horton is famous for another, less imposing historical monument. Villagers will direct you to a hedge beneath which the luckless Duke of Monmouth was discovered as he fled to the coast in 1685 after the Battle of Sedgemoor. Dressed as a poor shepherd he crawled exhausted into a ditch to sleep. When discovered he might have got away with the disguise, but the foolish man had in his pocket an item that no farmhand would possess — his badge of the Order of the Garter. Seven days later he was beheaded on Tower Hill.

A little further north is the ruined 14th-century church of Knowlton, standing in a circular earthwork built in the Bronze Age. Skeletons have been found which lead archaeologists to believe that human sacrifices took place there. Knowlton village was wiped out by the Black Death in 1485, and with no population to serve, the church fell into ruin. Although it has been tidied up and prepared as a picnic spot, you will probably feel somewhat uneasy in this awesome place.

From Knowlton a steep hill takes you down into Cranborne. The village itself has little to offer today, but this peaceful corner of Dorset was important in the past when it was garrisoned for troops protecting the kings who hunted over Cranborne Chase. A thousand years old, the village has a lovely manor house; it is not open to the public, but you see it when you visit the gardens.

The private gardens of this ancient manor, which was given to Robert Cecil (Queen Elizabeth's chief minister) by James I, and which is now lived in by his descendant the present Marquess of Salisbury, are open to the public on the first Saturday and Sunday of each month from April to October. They were laid out at the beginning of the 17th century by Mounten Jennings and John Tradescant who supplied many of the original plants.

More recently the garden was the scene of much of the filming of *Tom Jones*. Described as one of 'the great gardens of Great Britain', it contains a Jacobean mount garden, herb and wall gardens, a knot garden planted with flowers which were grown in the 16th and 17th centuries, a river garden, and daffodils, flowering cherries, fine avenues and yew hedges.

The garden centre caters for most of the needs of gardeners and, as well as many unusual plants, you will find roses, including species and old-fashioned, herbs, silver and grey foliage plants, shrubs, fruit trees, bedding and pot plants, bulbs, seeds, statuary and garden ornaments especially imported from Italy.

The house, now mainly Jacobean, was originally built as a hunting lodge in the reign of King John in 1207. It was then partially fortified and of very simple construction. The building consisted of a great hall with a central fireplace and a hole in the roof to let out the smoke, a buttery with an upper room and a chapel above approached by a ladder at one end. There was also an undercroft.

Around 1400 modifications to the building included the construction of the newel stair and the building of a tower. During this period, the principal owners were the Earls of Gloucester.

Early in the 17th century, King James I granted the manor to Robert Cecil, 1st Earl of Salisbury. As the house was almost in ruins, John Norden was employed to make a general survey of the property. Remodelling began in 1608 and continued to about 1636. New work included

Mowing the grass in Horton churchyard

Cranborne Manor

the east tower on the south side, the mullioned windows, the north and south porches, the Jacobean decorations on the buttresses and the south courtyard with its brick gatehouse. All the floor levels were altered and, in addition, an east wing and a west wing were added, but these no longer exist in their original form. The work was done by local craftsmen under the direction of William Arnold. During the Civil War much damage was done and, in 1647, a new west wing was built.

The Manor House is approached from the south through an archway flanked by two gatehouses, brick built. This became the main entrance in the 17th century, and this front has remained unaltered since that date. Above the 17th-century portico are the sculptured symbols of Libra and Virgo, and it is probable that the ten circular recesses below the second-storey windows were designed to contain other signs of the zodiac. During the renovations at the beginning of the 17th century, the battlements of the south-west tower were removed and its height was increased. At the south-east corner of the house a corresponding tower was built.

Cranborne Church

The north front is as altered in the Jacobean period. Originally the north door was the only entrance to the house. Above the porch, the sculptured coat of arms of the second Earl of Salisbury was added in 1647.

At the beginning of the 17th century, the garden was laid out formally but the parterres have since become lawns. The north and south courts were relaid in the 19th century and the former remains as then, except that it is filled with white flowering plants. The flower beds and cobbling in the south court were laid in the 1960s. It is considered one of Dorset's finest gardens.

The west garden is known as the mount garden because it retains its Jacobean mount. The east garden consists of the Church Walk and the old kitchen gardens. The Church Walk has spring bedding plants, followed by summer blooms; an apple tunnel leads off it. The herb garden was made in 1960, and contains many sweet-smelling plants.

The river garden is at the lower end of the north garden and stretches down to the river Crane. Plants and flowering shrubs give colour throughout the season. A garden with plants and flowering shrubs which were grown in the 16th and 17th centuries is known as the Elizabethan knot garden.

Cranborne House still belongs to the Cecil family who own the village. The church has a 13th-century nave but a Victorian chancel. It has a fine pulpit dating back to the early 15th century and there are remains of medieval wall paintings.

A chalk-capped earthwork just south-east of the village is believed to be Anglo-Saxon, but they say that a Mr Tregonwell buried his horse in it.

# WIMBORNE MINSTER

Priest's House Museum
open Easter Mon - end
Sept; weekdays 10.30-
12.30, 2.00-4.30

Price guide A

Wimborne is a pleasant little town, despite the intrusion of traffic which has caused it to be divided by one-way streets. Over 1000 years ago it was a town of some repute, the home of kings and the burial place of one of the most famous of Anglo-Saxon rulers, King Ethelred, slain by the Danes who came across the heath from Poole Harbour.

With its Minster dominating the town centre, Wimborne resembles a cathedral city in miniature. Romans settled the site and Anglo-Saxons built it up. In the 8th century Cuthberga, to whom the Minster is dedicated, founded a nunnery, which gave the town its ecclesiastical importance. The Danes made persistent raids on Wimborne in the 9th and 10th centuries and it was during one of these raids, in 871, that the king was killed. In the late 10th century, they also destroyed the nunnery.

Edward the Confessor revived the religious life by creating a college of secular canons. It was called a deanery under Henry III and, in 1318, Edward II declared the church a free chapel. It was dissolved in 1537.

Nothing is left of the collegiate buildings but the church has survived, having been restored in the 19th century. People gather on the lawns, before entering, to watch the 'Quarter Jack' high up on the north face of the west tower strike the quarter hours on the bells. Today the crudely painted effigy has the uniform of a 19th-century Grenadier, but when it was made in 1613 the striker was a monk.

The Minster

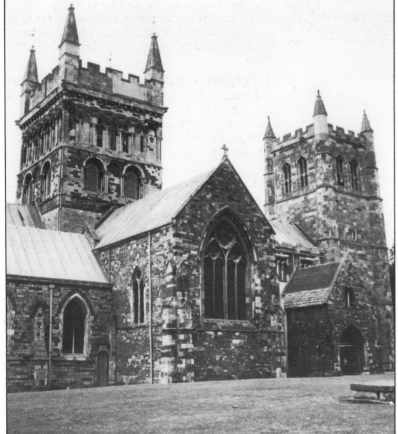

There is much to see in the Minster and you will need to invest in a guide book. The long nave has stately Norman pillars and the crossing tower rises nearly 100 feet, and carries a peal of ten bells.

The chained library

The chained library, which includes church-wardens' accounts since 1403, and 17th-century sermons, is a remarkable survival. Older than the 'Quarter Jack' is the orrery — a clockwork representation of the solar system — in a wall of the tower. The dial probably dates from the 15th century, but the present works were made by William Monk in 1740. The old clock has a blue background representing the sky. The sun, moon and stars revolve around our planet, with the sun completing its circuit in 24 hours, and the moon in a lunar month. The latter revolves on its axis shining gilt at full moon, gradually changing to dark. Two winged and trumpeting angels crown the dial.

The orrery - a clock which shows the Sun and Moon circling the Earth

The Minster has several splendid tombs but none more touching than a brass plate in the pavement recording Ethelred the Martyr, who lies beneath this spot. In the north choir aisle an unusually relaxed figure of a knight commemorates Sir Edmund Uvedale, 1606. This is considered to be the Minster's finest tomb and was erected by his widow as 'a doleful duty'. The excellent monument, with its background of alabaster, richly decorated, depicts Sir Edmund as if awakening from sleep.

All explorers will ask to see the strange resting place of Anthony Ettrick, a Recorder of Poole, who declared he would neither lie in or out of the Minster. he made his own coffin in oak and encased it in slate, pre-dating it 1691. He lived 12 years longer than he anticipated, and the date had to be altered when they carried out his wishes, placing his coffin in a niche in the wall so that he is neither underground or overground, neither in nor out. Ettrick was the magistrate to whom they brought the disguised Duke of Monmouth in 1685 when he was discovered in a ditch at Horton after the Battle of Sedgemoor. The Duke was beheaded in London a fortnight later.

There are many excellent windows but all are modern except the Tree of Jesus in the east window which is 15th-century.

Ancient chests in the Minster include one which is believed to have been the strong box of the Saxon nunnery. Over six feet long, the inner cavity is only 22 inches long, nine inches wide and six inches deep.

As you leave the Minster, look right past the war memorial and there is the ancient Priest's House, a medieval building much altered in the 17th and 18th centuries. It now serves as the town museum. Here you can see items of local history, with archaeological finds from a Bronze Age burial ground, and Romano-British relics. There is also a display of domestic Victoriana. At the rear, an extension has been opened for old rural bygones. You can walk in the garden too and see the mulberry tree, believed to be 300 years old. To provide variety, this museum also holds temporary exhibitions.

The Priest's House Gardens behind the museum

Wimborne Museum

To the left of the Minster's entrance, a narrow lane leads into the Cornmarket. Although dollied up now as a precinct, it is a reminder of the days when Wimborne was an important market town. One of two former Georgian inns — the White Hart — is still open, and displays a fixed iron rod to which convicts in transit could be handcuffed whilst the guards took refreshment.

The Dutch-gabled facade of the Oddfellows Hall of 1758 dominates the little square, but the stocks which were once set up there are now in the museum. The north-west corner gives access to the model town, a fascinating replica of Wimborne. School Lane on the other side of the Minster leads past the 18th-century chantry to the former Queen Elizabeth's Grammar School, rebuilt in 1849 using the Tudor style of the time of its origin.

A modern shopping precinct has been well hidden behind the old town and is part of a complex which includes police headquarters, courts and social services.

Near the Minster, in Dean's Walk Lane, is Dean's Court which, in spite of its nearness to the town centre, is in complete seclusion. This early Georgian house was built for Sir William

Hanham in 1725. It is on the site of the former deanery and the gardens, described as 'wild', are open to the public on Thursdays and Sundays from the end of May to September.

Although small, Wimborne has four interesting bridges; two over the Allen and two over the Stour. The oldest, Julian's Bridge, was built in 1636, but it still carries the flow of modern traffic toward Dorchester and the West. Walford over the Allen is an old packhorse bridge, and Eastbrook crosses the same river in the heart of the town. Canford Bridge, built in 1813, carries the Poole road on three bold arches of Portland stone.

Half a mile out of town, on the Badbury Rings road to Blandford (B3082), the St Margaret's Leper Hospital sits at the bottom of the hill. The medieval chapel is surrounded by thatched cottages, recently renovated, which are now almshouses.

One and a half miles south-east of Wimborne is a large Gothic mansion, formerly the home of the Wimbornes, and now a public school. A pleasant Stourside walk leads from the town to Canford School.

Julian's Bridge, built in 1636

# MERLEY BIRD GARDENS

Open summer 10.30-6.30;
winter 10.30-dusk

So many corners of Dorset have connections with the Civil War. We are aware, for instance, of the future Charles II's escapades in the west of the county, but it is more surprising to find reference to it in the peace of the Merley Bird Gardens near Wimborne.

These gardens, set in delightful surroundings, with lawns and open areas where you can bring a picnic and enjoy the sunshine, provide a thrilling display of some of the world's most exotic and beautiful birds. The various aviaries contain dozens of species, many from the tropics, ranging from tiny zebra finches and South American lorikeets to the brightly-coloured Amazonian parrots and macaws. Budgerigars and parakeets are very numerous, of course, and you'll also see picturesque lovebirds from Asia, Australian rosellas with their superb plumage, and also a talking magpie. Close by is the always-

It all began towards the end of the Civil War when an ardent Royalist, Ralph Willett, saw that his cause was lost and left for the West Indies, where he made a fortune in the sugar trade. Years later, his grandson returned to England and bought the Merley Estate in 1751.

popular dovecote and central fountain with separate pools for flamingoes and penguins. Not forgetting Lord Louis, the blue and yellow macaw, who wanders freely around the gardens. And that's only the beginning — there are scores of other interesting kinds of birds, and the new water gardens will delight people of every age.

As well as the gardens themselves, use is made of the other original estate buildings and landscape features. The superb orangery, for instance, has a spacious sun terrace where you can sit and enjoy a cool beer and a snack, and there is an excellent licensed restaurant inside serving a wide choice of English and European dishes accompanied by a selection of wines.

The Children's Corner with its rabbits, tortoises and other pets is extremely popular and the children's play area includes crazy golf and joy-rider mini-cars.

The house alone took eight years to build, and the young Ralph Willett oversaw the design and construction of a spacious walled garden at the same time. Fruit trees were set to grow, and row upon row of vegetables were planted to supply the fastidious tastes of the gentry who attended Ralph Willett's sumptuous banquets.

On the north side of the garden, he incorporated a 'pleasure area', with coloured hempen hammocks slung between the trees, and quiet walks laid out along arcades of sweet-smelling roses. Opposite this area, on the south side of the garden, he built the magnificent orangery, whose facade still remains as a fine example of artistic bricklaying.

This walled garden is the site of the Merley Bird Gardens, which were set up in 1968. The present owners, the Martin family from Poole, have been there since 1981.

Another special feature is the Tree Walk, laid out along one side of the walled garden. This walk, laid out and planted in the 18th century as part of the original estate design, has now been restored to its original form. The Merley area may not be the most beautiful part of Dorset but, once inside this walled garden, you will absorb the peaceful atmosphere of an old estate while experiencing something of the colour and excitement of exotic lands.